W9-ATC-655

MIPS RISC Architecture

This book describes the MIPS RISC Architecture.
The R2000 Processor and R2010 Floating Point Accelerator
are the original implementation of the architecture and
the R2000/R2010 numbering notation is used throughout the text.
Higher-performance versions of the two machines,
the R3000 and R3010, are the newest implementation of
the MIPS RISC architecture. All references in this book
to the R2000/R2010 Processors apply fully
to the new R3000/R3010 Processors.

Gerry Kane

Prentice Hall, Englewood Cliffs, NJ 07632

Library of Congress Catalog Card Number 88-060290

© 1987, 1988, 1989. MIPS Computer Systems, Inc. All Rights Reserved. No part of this document may be reproduced in any form or by any means without prior express written consent of MIPS Computer Systems, Inc., and the publisher.

The information contained in this book is for reference only and is subject to change without notice.

RISComputer, RISC/os, and RISCompilers are Trademarks of MIPS Computer Systems.
UNIX is a Trademark of AT&T.
Ethernet is a Trademark of XEROX.
VAX is a Trademark of Digital Equipment Corp.
IBM is a Trademark of International Business Machines.
68000 is a Trademark of Motorola Semiconductor Corp.

Book Design: Suzanne Hayes-Kane.

The publisher offers discounts on this book when ordered in bulk quantities. For more information, write:
    Special Sales/College Marketing
    Prentice-Hall, Inc.
    College Technical and Reference Division
    Englewood Cliffs, NJ 07632

All rights reserved. No part of this book may be reproduced, in any form or by any means, without permission in writing from the publisher.

Printed in the United States of America

10 9 8 7

ISBN   0-13-584293-X
ISBN   0-13-584749-4 {PH}

Prentice-Hall International (UK) Limited, *London*
Prentice-Hall of Australia Pty. Limited, *Sydney*
Prentice-Hall Canada Inc., *Toronto*
Prentice-Hall Hispanoamericana, S.A., *Mexico*
Prentice-Hall of India Private Limited, *New Delhi*
Prentice-Hall of Japan, Inc., *Tokyo*
Simon & Schuster Asia Pte. Ltd., *Singapore*
Editora Prentice-Hall do Brasil, Ltda., *Rio de Janeiro*

Acknowledgements

The following folks from MIPS Computer Systems contributed valuable suggestions that improved the accuracy and readability of this book: John Moussouris, Larry Weber, John Mashey, Earl Killian, Edward (Skip) Stritter. Special credit goes to Craig Hansen who wrote the original architectural specifications that served as the source material for this book.

Personal thanks go to the usual suspects: Suzanne, Sean, Kyle, Ambrose, Marcella.

This book is dedicated to the memory of RedBob (Robert A. Knox), a source of joy and energy to all who knew him. Perhaps not the soul of the MIPS machine—but certainly, the wit. He is greatly missed.

Organization

This book is organized into two major sections: Chapters 1 through 5 describe the characteristics of the R2000 Processor and Chapters 6, 7, and 8 describe the R2010 FPA. The contents of each chapter are summarized in the list that follows:

- **Chapter 1, RISC Architecture: An Overview,** describes the general characteristics and concepts of reduced instruction set computers.

- **Chapter 2, R2000 Processor Overview,** describes the general characteristics and capabilities of the processor. It also provides a programming model which describes how data is represented in the R2000 registers and in memory and also provides a summary of the R2000 CPU registers.

- **Chapter 3, Instruction Set Summary,** provides a summary description of the R2000 instruction set.

- **Chapter 4, Memory Management System,** describes the virtual memory system supported by the R2000's System Control Coprocessor.

- **Chapter 5, Exception Processing,** describes the events that cause R2000 exceptions and the sequences that occur during processing of the exceptions.

- **Chapter 6, R2010 FPA Overview,** describes the general characteristics and capabilities of the FPA. This chapter also provides a summary of the R2010 FPA registers and describes how data is represented in the R2010 registers.

- **Chapter 7, FPA Instruction Summary & Instruction Pipeline,** provides a summary description of the R2010 instruction set and a discussion of instruction overlapping.

- **Chapter 8, Floating Point Exceptions,** describes how the R2010 FPA supports the IEEE standard floating point exceptions.

- **Appendix A** provides a detailed description of the format and operation of each R2000 instruction.

- **Appendix B** provides a detailed description of the format and operation of each R2010 FPA instruction.

- **Appendix C** describes machine language programming tips that can simplify implementation of commonly required tasks.

- **Appendix D** describes assembly language programming techniques and provides guidelines for writing programs for use with the MIPS assembler.

- **Appendix E** describes how the R2010 FPA supports the IEEE floating point standard and provides programming tips that can simplify implementation of standard operations not implemented by the FPA.

About This Book

This book is a comprehensive reference manual for the MIPS RISC architecture. It describes the functional characteristics and capabilities of the R2000/R3000 Processors and the R2010/R3010 Floating Point Accelerators (FPA). The new, higher-performance R3000/R3010 machines are architecturally identical to the original R2000/R2010 versions and the descriptions in this book apply to both series of machines — only the electrical and performance characteristics differ. The processors are available from the following manufacturers:

- Integrated Device Technology, Inc.
  3226 Scott Boulevard
  P.O. Box Box 58015
  Santa Clara, CA 95054-3029
  (408) 727-6116
  Telex 887766
  FAX (408) 988-3029

- LSI Logic Corporation
  1551 McCarthy Blvd.
  MS D-105
  Milpitas, CA 95035
  (408) 433-8000
  Telex 171.641
  FAX (408) 433-3816
  Attn: Standard Products Marketing

- MIPS Computer Systems, Inc.
  930 Arques Avenue
  Sunnyvale, CA 94086-3650
  (408) 720-1700
  Telex 510 601 5346
  FAX (408) 720-9809

- Performance Semiconductor Corporation
  610 E. Weddell Drive
  Sunnyvale, CA 94089
  (408) 734-9000
  FAX (408) 734-0258
  Attn: Microprocessor Marketing

- NEC Electronics, Inc.
  401 Ellis Street
  P.O. Box 7241
  Mountain View, CA
  (415) 960-6000
  Attn: Microprocessor Marketing

- Siemens Components, Inc.
  2191 Laurelwood Road
  Santa Clara, CA 95054
  (408) 980-4500
  Attn: Integrated Circuits Division

Contents

2
R2000 Processor Overview

3
R2000 Instruction Set Summary

4
Memory Management System

5
Exception Processing

6

R2010 FPA Overview

7
FPA Instruction Set Summary
& Instruction Pipeline

8
Floating Point Exceptions

A
R2000 Instruction Set Details

B
R2010 FPA Instruction Set Details

C
Machine Language Programming Tips

D
Assembly Language Programming

E
IEEE Floating Point Standard Compatibility Issues

Index

RISC Architecture: An Overview

The MIPS R2000 RISC architecture delivers dramatic cost/performance advantages over computers based on traditional architectures. This advantage is the result of a development methodology that demands optimization across many disciplines including custom VLSI, CPU organization, system–level architecture, operating system considerations, and compiler design. The trade–offs involved in this optimization process typify, and indeed are the essence of, RISC design. Although most of this book is devoted to describing the R2000 architecture, this chapter provides a context for that description by examining some of the underlying concepts that characterize RISC architectures in general.

Scope of this Overview

RISC design is a methodology still in its infancy, enduring the usual growing pains as it strives for maturity. Because of the complexity of the subject and its dynamic state, a thorough and comprehensive discussion is beyond the scope of this book. A concise discussion of RISC is made more difficult by the nature of the design techniques — they involve myriad trade-offs and compromises between software/hardware, silicon area/compiler technology, component process technology/system software requirements, and so on. Therefore, this chapter provides only a brief overview of RISC concepts and their implementation so that the architecture of the MIPS R2000 processors can be better understood and appreciated.

What Is RISC?

The evolution of computer architectures was dominated, until recently, by families of increasingly complex processors. Under market pressures to preserve existing software, complex instruction set computer (CISC) architectures evolved by the gradual addition of microcode and increasingly elaborate operations. The intent was to supply more support for high–level languages and operating systems, as semiconductor advances made it possible to fabricate more complex integrated circuits. It seemed self–evident that architectures *should* become more complex as technology advances made it possible to include more complexity on VLSI devices.

In recent years, however, reduced instruction set computer (RISC) architectures have implemented a much more sophisticated division of complexity between hardware, firmware, and software. RISC concepts emerged from statistical analysis of how software actually uses the resources of a processor. Dynamic measurement of system kernels and object modules generated by optimizing compilers show an overwhelming predominance, even in the code for CISC machines, of the simplest instructions. Complex instructions are seldom used because microcode rarely provides the precise routines needed to support a variety of high–level–language and system environments. Therefore, RISC designs eliminate the microcoded routines and turn the low–level control of the machine over to software.

This approach is not new. But its application is more universal in recent years thanks to the prevalence of high–level languages, the development of compilers that can optimize at the "microcode" level, and dramatic advances in semiconductor memory and packaging. It is now feasible to replace a machine's microcode ROM with faster RAM organized as an instruction cache. Machine control then resides in the instruction cache and is, in effect, customized on the fly. The instruction stream generated by system and compiler–generated code provides a precise fit between the requirements of high–level software and the capabilities of the hardware.

Notice that reducing or simplifying the instruction set is not the primary goal of the architectural concepts described here — it is really just a side effect of the techniques used to obtain the highest performance possible from available technology. Thus, the term *Reduced Instruction Set Computers* is a bit misleading: it is the push for performance that really drives and shapes RISC designs. Therefore, let us begin by defining performance.

Defining Performance

The performance of a processor can be defined as the time required to accomplish a specific task (or program, or algorithm, or benchmark) and can be expressed as the product of three factors:

$$Time\ per\ Task\ =\ C\ *\ T\ *\ I$$
$$where:\quad C\ =\ Cycles\ per\ Instructions$$
$$T\ =\ Time\ per\ Cycle\ (clock\ speed)$$
$$I\ =\ Instructions\ per\ Task$$

Performance can be improved by reducing any of these three factors. RISC–type designs strive to improve performance by minimizing the first two factors. However, changes that reduce the cycles/instruction and time/cycle factors tend to increase the instructions/task factor: this tendency has been the focus of most criticisms leveled at RISC. However, the use of optimizing compilers and other techniques mitigate this tendency. The sections that follow discuss each of the three performance–related factors and typical techniques used in RISC–type designs to minimize each factor.

Time per Instruction

The time required to execute an instruction is the product of the first two factors (C and T) in the equation developed in the preceding section. These two factors are complementary: increasing the clock speed (reducing the time per cycle) decreases the amount of work that can be accomplished within a cycle. Thus, fast clock rates (short cycle times) tend to increase the number of cycles required to perform an instruction as illustrated in the following figure:

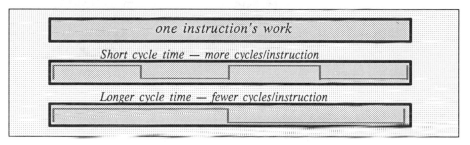

In most processors, it makes little difference whether cycle time is short and instructions require many cycles, or cycle time is long with instructions requiring few cycles — it's the total time/instruction (time/cycle X cycles/instruction) that is significant. Typically, the cycle time is chosen to allow execution of the most simple operations (or sub–operations) in a single cycle, and execution of other, more complex operations in multiple cycles. Thus, the instruction stream in a typical CISC processor might look like this:

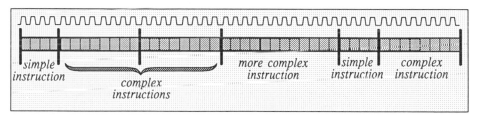

Executing the most simple instructions in the above example requires four cycles and executing the more complex instruction requires eight or twelve cycles. This approach would seem to achieve a rather efficient utilization of time: simple instructions are executed quickly and more complicated instructions are given additional time to execute. Each instruction is given just the amount of time it needs — no more and no less. This technique has one very damaging drawback, however, that makes it unsuitable in RISC–type designs: it greatly complicates the use of instruction pipelines. Instruction pipelines are an essential technique used to reduce the cycles/instruction factor, and the gains that pipelines can provide are negated by instruction sets where the cycles/instruction factor is variable. The advantages of instruction pipelines and the impact that their use has on the design of instruction sets are discussed in the sections that follow.

Cycles per Instruction (C)

If the work that each instruction performs is simple and straightforward, then the time required to execute each instruction can be shortened and the number of cycles reduced. The goal of RISC designs is to achieve an execution rate of one machine cycle per instruction. Techniques that allow this goal to be approached include:

- Instruction pipelines
- Load/Store architecture
- Delayed load instructions
- Delayed branch instructions

Instruction Pipelines

One way to reduce the number of cycles required to execute an instruction is to overlap the execution of multiple instructions. Instruction pipelines work by dividing the execution of each instruction into several discrete portions and then executing multiple instructions simultaneously. For example, the execution of an instruction might be subdivided into four portions as shown below:

Cycle #1	Cycle #2	Cycle #3	Cycle #4
Fetch Instruction (F)	ALU Operation (A)	Access Memory (M)	Write Results (W)

In this example, four clock cycles are required to execute an instruction. An instruction pipeline, however, can *potentially* reduce the number of cycles/instruction by a factor equal to the depth of the pipeline. For example, in the following figure, each instruction still requires a total of four clock cycles to execute. However, if a four–level instruction pipeline is used, a new instruction can be initiated at each clock cycle and the effective execution rate is one cycle per instruction. The instruction pipeline technique can be likened to an assembly line — the instruction progresses from one specialized stage to the next until it is completed just as an automobile might move along an assembly line. This is in contrast to the non–pipeline, microcoded approach where all the work is done by one general unit, which is less capable at each individual task.

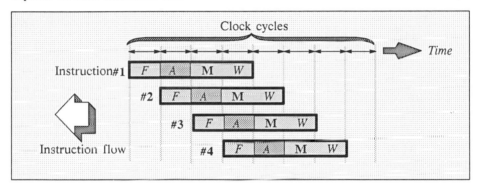

Note that the previous paragraph stated that a pipeline can *potentially* reduce the number of cycles/instruction by a factor equal to the depth of the pipeline. Fulfilling this potential requires that the pipeline always be filled with useful instructions and that nothing delay the advance of instructions through the pipeline. These requirements impose certain demands on the architecture. For example, consider the earlier example of serially executing an instruction stream where each instruction can require a different number of clock cycles. The following figure illustrates how this instruction stream might look as it proceeds through a pipeline:

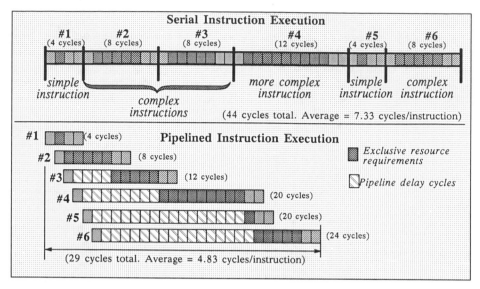

In this example, the darkly-shaded cycles indicate those where the instructions require the use of the same resources (for example, the ALU, shifters, or registers). Competition for these resources blocks the progression of the instructions through the pipeline and causes delay cycles to be inserted for many of the instructions until the required resources become available. The pipeline technique shortens the average number of cycles/instruction in this example, but the gains are greatly reduced by the delay cycles that must be added.

The negative effect of the variable execution times is actually much worse than the simple preceding example might indicate. Management of an instruction pipeline requires proper and efficient handling of events such as branches, exceptions or interrupts that can completely disrupt the flow of instructions. If the instruction stream can include a variety of different instruction lengths and a mixture of delay and normal cycles, pipeline management becomes very complex. Additionally, such a varied, complex instruction stream makes it almost impossible for a compiler to schedule instructions so as to reduce or eliminate delays. It is for these reasons that a primary goal of RISC designs is to define an instruction set where execution of all, or most, instructions requires a uniform number of cycles and, ideally, to achieve a rate of execution of one cycle/instruction.

Load/Store Architecture

The discussion of the instruction pipeline illustrated how each instruction can be subdivided into several discrete parts which then permit the processor to execute multiple instructions in parallel. For this technique to work efficiently, the time required to execute each instruction sub-part should be approximately equal. If one part requires an excessive length of time, then all the cycles must be made longer or additional cycles must be used for the longer operation.

Instructions that perform operations on operands in memory tend to increase either the cycle time or the number of cycles/instruction. Such instructions require additional time for execution to calculate the addresses of the operands, read the required operands from memory, calculate the result, and store the results of the operation back to memory. To eliminate the negative impact of such instructions, RISC designs implement a *Load/Store* architecture in which all operations are performed on operands held in processor registers, and main memory is accessed only by load and store instructions. This approach produces several benefits:

- reducing the number of memory accesses eases memory bandwidth requirements

- limiting all operations to registers helps simplify the instruction set

- eliminating memory operations makes it easier for compilers to optimize register allocation — this further reduces memory accesses and also reduces the instructions/task factor.

All of these factors help RISC designs approach their goal of executing one cycle/instruction. However, two classes of instructions still inhibit reaching this goal — load instructions and branch instructions. The sections that follow discuss how RISC designs overcome obstacles raised by these classes of instructions.

Delayed Load Instructions

Load instructions read operands from memory into processor registers for subsequent operation by other instructions. Because memory typically operates at much slower speeds than processor clock rates, the *loaded* operand is not immediately available to subsequent instructions in a processor with an instruction pipeline. This data dependency situation is illustrated in the following figure:

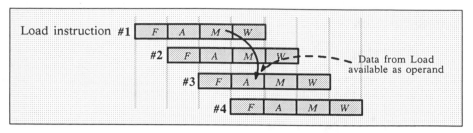

In this illustration, the operand loaded by instruction #1 is not available in time for use in the "A" cycle of instruction #2. One way to handle this dependency is to delay the pipeline by inserting additional clock cycles into the execution of instruction #2 until the loaded data becomes available. This approach would obviously introduce delays that would increase the cycles/instruction factor.

The technique used in many RISC designs to handle this data dependency is to recognize and make visible to compilers the fact that all load instructions inherently have a latency or load delay. In the preceding illustration, there is a load delay or latency of one instruction. The instruction that immediately follows the load is described as being in the *load delay slot*. If the instruction that is in this slot does not require the data from the load, then no delay of the pipeline is required.

If the existence of this load delay is made visible to software, a compiler can arrange instructions to ensure that there is no data dependency between a load instruction and the instruction in the load delay slot. The simplest way of ensuring that there is no data dependency is to insert a NOP (No Operation) instruction to fill the slot:

```
Load    R1,A
Load    R2,B
NOP            <-- this instruction fills the delay slot
Add     R3,R1,R2
```

Although it eliminates the need for hardware-controlled pipeline stalls in this case, filling the delay slot with NOP instructions still is not a very efficient use of the pipeline stream since the NOP instructions increase the code size and perform no useful work. (In practice, however, this technique need not have much negative impact on performance, especially if the delay is only one cycle.)

A more effective solution to handling the data dependency situation is to fill the load delay slot with a useful instruction. Good optimizing compilers can usually accomplish this, especially if the load delay is only one instruction. The following figure illustrates how a compiler might rearrange instructions to handle a potential data dependency:

```
# Consider the code for C := A+ B; F := D
   Load     R1,A
   Load     R2,B
   Add      R3,R1,R2   <-- this instruction stalls because R2 data is not available
   Load     R4,D
   ...      ...
# An alternative code sequence (where delay length = 1)
   Load     R1,A
   Load     R2,B
   Load     R4,D
   Add      R3,R1,R2   <-- no stall since R2 data is available
   ...      ...
```

Since the Add (Add R3,R1,R2) instruction does not depend on the availability of the data from the third Load instruction (Load R4,D), the delay slot (for Load R2,B) can be filled with a usable instruction (Load R4,D) and the pipeline can be fully utilized.

Delayed Branch Instructions

Branch instructions usually delay the instruction pipeline because the processor must calculate the effective destination of the branch and fetch that instruction. When a cache access requires an entire cycle, and the fetched branch instruction specifies the target address, it is impossible to perform this fetch (of the destination instruction) without delaying the pipeline for at least one pipe stage (one cycle). Conditional branches may cause further delays because they require the calculation of a condition, as well as the target address. The following figure illustrates a delay of one pipeline stage while the instruction at the destination address is calculated and fetched:

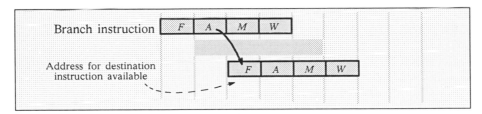

Instead of stalling the instruction pipeline to wait for the instruction at the target address, RISC designs typically use an approach similar to that used with Load instructions: Branch instructions are delayed and do not take effect until after one or more instructions immediately following the Branch instruction have been executed. The instruction or instructions in this branch delay slot are always executed, as illustrated in the following figure.

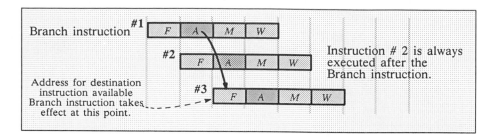

With this approach, the inherent delay associated with the branch instructions is made visible to the software, and compilers attempt to fill the branch delay slot with useful instructions. This task is usually not too difficult if there is only a one in-struction delay as is the case in the following code example:

Typical CISC-type code	RISC-type code with delayed branches	RISC-type code with delay slots filled

A: move s0,a0
   move s1,a1
   addiu s0,s0,1
   beq   s0,zero,D
	A: move s0,a0
	   move s1,a1
	   addiu s0,s0,1
	   beq s0,zero,D
	   nop <- delay slot
		A: move s0,a0
		
		   addiu s0,s0,1
		   beq s0,zero,D
		   move s1,a1 <- moved from above

B: move a0,s0
   move a1,s1
	B: move a0,s0
	   move a1,s1
		move a0,s0 ————————————

C: jal X	C: jal X
	   nop <- delay slot
		C: jal X
		   move a1,s1 <- moved from above

addiu s0,s0,1
   bne   s0,zero,B
	addiu s0,s0,1
	   bne s0,zero,B
	   nop <- delay slot
		addiu s0,s0,1
		   bne s0,zero,C <- orig. target + 4
		   move a0,s0 <- dup. target instr.

D: --	D: --	D: --

If the branch delay slot cannot be filled with any useful instructions, NOP instruc-tions can be inserted to keep the instruction pipeline filled. Usually, however, a compiler can fill the slot with useful instructions. The preceding example illustrates two different techniques used to fill the slot:

- Often, an instruction that occurs before the branch can be executed after the branch without affecting the logic or the Branch instruction itself. Thus, in the example, the *move s1,a1* and *move a1,s1* instruc-tions can be moved from their original positions to the delay slots without changing the logic of the program.

- The original target instruction of the *bne* instruction was the *move a0,s0* instruction at label *B:*. In the example, this instruction is duplicated in the delay slot following the *bne* instruction and the target of the *bne* instruction is changed to be the instruction at label *C:*. Note that while this technique increases the static number of instructions by one, it does not increase the dynamic instruction count: the same number of instructions are executed during the program as in the CISC–type code illustrated in the example.

Time per Cycle (T)

The time required to perform a single machine cycle is determined by such factors as:

- Instruction decode time.
- Instruction operation time.
- Instruction access time (memory bandwidth).
- Architectural simplicity.

Many of the same design approaches that reduce the number of cycles/instruction also help reduce the time/cycle. For example, dividing up an instruction's execution into several discrete stages to implement the instruction pipeline can also result in reducing the time required to execute a cycle.

Instruction Decode Time

The time required to decode instructions is partly related to the number of instructions in the instruction set and the variety of instruction formats supported. Thus, simple, uniform RISC instruction sets minimize the instruction decode circuitry and time requirements. For example, if the instruction formats are uniform, with consistent use of bit fields within the instructions, then the processor can decode multiple fields simultaneously to speed the process. In addition to providing instructions only to perform simple tasks, RISC designs also reduce the number of options such as addressing modes to further reduce the number of possible instruction formats.

Instruction Operation Time

For CISC architectures, instruction operation time is usually measured in multiples of cycles. RISC designs, however, strive to make all instructions execute within a single cycle and, further, to make that cycle time as short as possible. Many of the techniques discussed earlier under the category of reducing the number of cycles/instruction also help reduce instruction operation time. For example, the time required for register–to–register operations is much less than the time needed to operate on memory operands. Thus, the load/store architectural approach described earlier also helps reduce the cycle time.

Instruction Access Time (Memory Bandwidth)

The time needed to access (fetch) an instruction is largely a function of the memory system supported and often becomes the limiting factor in RISC–type designs because of the high rate at which instructions can be executed. While the load/store architecture (discussed earlier in this chapter) common to RISC designs helps reduce memory bandwidth requirements, achieving an execution rate of one cycle/instruction is impossible unless the memory system can deliver instructions at the cycle rate of the processor. A variety of techniques are used to obtain the required memory bandwidth needed to support the high–performance RISC designs. Two common techniques are:

- Supporting hierarchical memory systems using high–speed cache memory to provide the primary, re–usable pool of instructions and data that are frequently accessed by the processor. Figure 1.1 illustrates the functional position of cache memory in a hierarchical memory system.

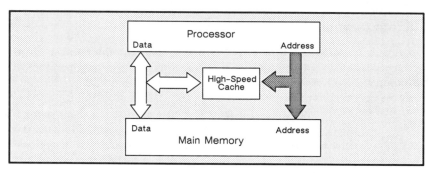

Figure 1.1   Functional Position of Cache in a Hierarchical Memory System

- Supporting separate caches for instructions and data to double the effective cache memory bandwidth. The access time of the cache memory devices can be the factor limiting the processor's throughput; the use of separate caches lets the processor alternate accesses between instruction cache and data cache. Figure 1.2 illustrates a memory system with separate caches for instructions and data.

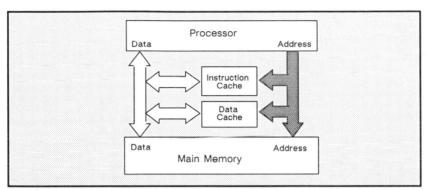

Figure 1.2 An R2000 System with a High–Performance Memory System

The use of separate caches for data and instructions has an additional benefit beyond decreasing the access time: the locality of a set of instructions or a set of data is typically much higher than that of a mixture of instructions and data. Therefore, for most programs, data and instructions held in separate caches are more likely to be re–usable than if a common, shared cache were used.

Another technique that helps minimize the time required to fetch an instruction is to require that all instructions be of a uniform length (a fixed number of bits) and that they always be aligned on a regular boundary. For example, many RISC processors define all instructions to be 32 bits wide and require that they be aligned on word boundaries. This approach eliminates the possibility of a single instruction extending across a word boundary (requiring multiple fetches) or across a memory management boundary (requiring multiple address translations).

Overall Architectural Simplicity

The general simplicity of RISC architectures allows streamlining of the entire machine's organization. As a result, the overhead on each instruction can be reduced and the clock cycle can be shortened, as designers are able to focus on optimizing a small number of critical processor features. The general simplicity of the machine also allows the use of more aggressive semiconductor process technologies in the manufacture of the processor. More aggressive process technologies provide the potential for faster performance.

Instructions per Task (I)

This factor of the performance equation is the one where RISC designs are most vulnerable and has been the source of most of the criticisms that were initially directed at RISC designs. Since RISC processors implement the more complex operations performed by CISC processors using a series of simple instructions, the total number of instructions required to perform a given task tends to increase as the complexity of the instruction set decreases. Therefore, a given program or algorithm written using the instruction set for a RISC processor tends to have more instructions than the same task written using the instruction set for a CISC processor.

However, advances in RISC techniques has done much to mitigate this negative tendency and, for many algorithms, the dynamic instruction count for good RISC processors is not significantly different than for CISC processors. The primary techniques that help reduce the instructions/task factor are:

- Optimizing compilers
- Operating system support

Optimizing Compilers

Reliance on high–level languages (HLL) has been increasing for many years while the importance of assembly language programming has diminished. This trend has led to an emphasis on the use of efficient compilers to convert HLL instructions to machine instructions. Primary measures of a compiler's efficiency are the compactness of the code it generates and the execution time of that code. Modern, optimizing compilers have evolved to provide great efficiency in the HLL–to–machine language translation.

There is nothing about optimizing compilers that is inherently RISC–oriented; many of the techniques they use were developed before the current generation of RISC architectures arrived and are applied to RISC and CISC machines alike. There is, however, a synergistic relationship between optimizing compilers and RISC architectures — compilers can do their best job of optimization with a RISC architecture, and RISC–type computers, in many cases, rely on compilers to obtain their full performance capabilities.

During the development of more efficient compilers, an analysis of instruction streams revealed that most time was spent executing simple instructions and performing load and store operations — more complex instructions were little used. It was also learned that compilers produced code that was often a narrow subset of a processor's architecture: complex instructions and features were not usable by compilers.

It might seem illogical that people writing compilers would end up ignoring the most powerful instructions and preferring the simpler ones, but it happens because the powerful instructions are hard for a compiler to use or because the instructions don't precisely fit the HLL requirements. A compiler prefers instructions that perform simple, well-defined operations with minimum side-effects. Since these characteristics are typical of a RISC instruction set, there is a natural match between RISC architectures and efficient, optimizing compilers. This match makes it easier for compilers to choose the most effective sequences of a machine's instructions to accomplish the tasks described by a high-level language.

Optimizing Techniques An examination of some of the techniques that compilers use to optimize programs will make the match between compilers and RISC architectures more apparent.

- *Register allocation.* The compiler allocates processor registers to hold frequently used data and thus reduce the number of load/store operations. The following simple example illustrates how careful register allocation can reduce the number of instructions required to perform a task:

```
# task is A:= B + C
    Load    R1,B
    Load    R2,C
    Add     R3,R1,R2
    Store   R3,A

# If A, B, and C are allocated to registers
    Add     Ra,Rb,Rc
```

  In this simple example, the two Load instructions are eliminated since the required values are already available in registers and the Store instruction is not needed since the compiler will hold the result of the Add in a register for future use.

- *Redundancy elimination.* The compiler looks for opportunities to reuse results and thus eliminate redundant computations.

- *Loop optimization.* A compiler optimizes loop operations by recognizing variables and expressions that don't change during a loop and moving them outside the loop.

- *Replace slow operations with faster ones.* A compiler searches for situations where slow operations, such as special cases of a multiply or divide, can be replaced with faster operations, such as shift and add instructions.

- *Strength reduction.* This technique consists of replacing "expensive" operations with cheaper ones. For example, multi–dimension arrays are often indexed using a combination of several multiplication and addition operations. Strength reduction might simplify the index calculation by using a previously calculated address and a simple addition operation.

- *Pipeline scheduling.* The compiler schedules and reorganizes instructions to ensure that pipeline delay slots are filled with useful instructions as illustrated earlier in the description of load and branch delays.

Again note that none of the techniques described above are uniquely linked to RISC architectures. However, the simplicity of a RISC machine makes it inherently easier for a compiler to discover optimization opportunities and implement these optimizations with a clear view of their effects.

Optimization Levels The development of optimizing compilers has produced its own terminology. This section describes the terms commonly used to categorize the various levels of optimization performed by compilers. The optimization techniques used can be divided into four levels according to their scope and degree of difficulty:

- *Peephole optimization* attempts to make improvements in code size or performance within a narrow context. An example of this level is replacing slower operations with faster ones.

- *Local optimization* makes decisions based on views of multiple–instruction sequences. An example of this level is to examine sequences of instructions to determine the best prologue/epilogue to use as the entry/exit code for a function. Other examples include keeping values in registers over short periods of time, and eliminating branch instructions whose target is another branch instruction.

- *Global optimization* optimizes program control flow by enhancing branch and loop structures and by performing strength reduction.

- *Inter–procedural optimization* This level is rarely performed because techniques like the following are just being developed:

  □ Allocating register assignments to maximize their life between procedures.

  □ Merging procedures and converting appropriate procedures to in–line code to reduce overhead.

Operating System Support

The performance gains obtained by providing support for operating systems are often subtle and not as easily defined or measured as with some of the other RISC techniques. While CISC architectures typically provide elaborate support for operating systems, the RISC approach emphasizes *appropriate* support. The appropriateness is based on a rigorous evaluation of the performance gains that can be obtained by the support of any particular function. The guiding principles are to avoid unnecessary complexity unless justified by statistics of actual usage, and to simplify and streamline operations required most frequently by operating systems.

The learning path here parallels the one traveled during exploration of compiler efficiencies — trying to put features supporting high-level languages into hardware often frustrated compiler writers. Similarly, putting special features into hardware to support operating systems does not always match the real needs of operating systems. With compilers, it was learned that the special instructions intended to simplify support of high-level languages were not often used by compilers. Similarly, it has been found that special hardware features for operating systems may also miss their mark. Often, the most efficient way of supporting an operating system is to just provide it with raw speed and with simple, minimal controls.

The paragraphs that follow illustrate some of the subtle ways in which RISC-type designs can supply appropriate operating system support to enhance performance without adding unacceptable complexity to the hardware:

Virtual Memory System. Translation Lookaside Buffers (TLBs) provide the virtual-to-physical address translation that is essential to implementing a powerful operating system. While there is nothing about TLBs that is RISC-specific, the chip area gained by overall simplification of the processor can be used to implement (larger) on-chip TLBs. An on-chip TLB enhances performance by eliminating the cycle(s) otherwise required to transfer the virtual address to an external TLB.

Modes And Protection. Operating systems require some mechanisms for controlling user access to system and processor resources. CISC processors often provide a variety of operating modes and protection mechanisms. Multiple modes and protection schemes add complexity to the hardware, however, and experience teaches that there is seldom a complete match between these mechanisms and operating system requirements. The RISC approach is to supply limited control and protection mechanisms: a simple kernel/privileged, user/unprivileged mode differentiation is usually sufficient. More elaborate schemes can then be implemented as needed in the kernel software.

Interrupts And Traps. Many CISC processors provide extensive hardware support for responding to interrupts and traps by saving a lot of state information and by generating numerous vector addresses to which control is transferred in response to exceptions. This support adds complexity to the hardware but does not necessarily produce corresponding simplification of the operating system's tasks. For example, many operating systems do not really need or use numerous distinct exception vector addresses: instead, they first execute a common interrupt handler which then does the work to determine the specific processing needed for the exception. The operating system itself might then determine what state information (if any) needs to be saved. This approach results in simplified hardware and lets the appropriate complexity be provided by the operating system as needed.

Special-function Instructions. Note that we have made no mention of special instructions to simplify and support operating system activities. Once again, the rule of simplicity and appropriateness argues against the inclusion of special instructions. Even in cases where significant time is spent in an operating system, the bulk of the time is spent executing general code rather than performing special functions. Thus, it is more efficient to let the operating system use the standard, simple, non-specialized instructions to perform all of its functions.

The RISC Design Process

The RISC design process is, at its best, an iterative process that uses feedback to tune the design. For example, MIPS Computer Systems started with the knowledge of earlier RISC efforts, including especially the Stanford University MIPS research work, and also started with the optimizing compilers from that effort. Based on that previous experience, a base-level instruction set was proposed, and measurements were taken from simulations of code compiled with the existing optimizers. Proposals for additions to the instruction set were carefully weighed to verify that they *actually* improved performance. Specifically, MIPS used the rule that any instruction added for performance reasons had to provide a verifiable 1% performance gain over a range of applications or else the instruction was rejected.

The result of this approach is an instruction set that is very well-tuned for high-level language use. Every instruction is either structurally necessary (such as Restore From Exception) or can naturally be generated by compilers. This stands in contrast to many other machines, even ones also labeled RISC, that often have user-level instructions or instruction mode combinations that are very difficult to reach from compiled languages.

These same stringent requirements were applied to the many different memory-management alternatives that were proposed and simulated before the final design for the R2000 was chosen. All functions and features which complicated the design had to be empirically proven to be performance enhancing within the complete system concept before they might be included.

Hidden Benefits of RISC Design

Some of the important benefits that results from the RISC design techniques are not attributable to the architectural characteristics adopted to enhance performance but are a result of the overall reduction in complexity: the simpler design allows both chip–area resources and human resources to be applied to features that enhance performance.

Shorter Design Cycle

The simplified architectures of RISC processors can be implemented more quickly: it is much easier to implement and debug a streamlined, simplified architecture with no microcode than a complex, microcoded architecture. CISC processors have such a long design cycle that they are often not fully debugged until the technology in which they were designed is obsolete. The shorter time required to design and implement RISC processors lets them make use of the best available technologies.

Smaller Chip Size

The simplicity of RISC processors also frees scarce chip–area resources for performance–critical structures like larger register files, translation–lookaside–buffers (TLB's), coprocessors, and fast multiply–divide units. These additional resources help these processors obtain an even greater performance edge.

User (Programmer) Benefits

Somewhat surprisingly, simplicity in architecture also helps the user:

- The uniform instruction set is easier to use.
- There is a closer correlation between instruction count and cycle count making it much easier to measure the true impact of code optimization activities.
- Programmers can have a higher confidence in hardware correctness.

Most Aggressive Semiconductor Technologies

Finally, as new VLSI implementation technologies are developed, they are always introduced with tight limits on the number of transistors than can fit on each chip.

The simplicity of a RISC architecture allows it to be implemented in far fewer transistors than CISC architectures. The result is that the first computers capable of exploiting the new VLSI technologies (for example, VLSI ECL, VLSI GaAs) will use RISC architectures. Therefore, RISC processors can always use the most advanced technologies and reap the performance benefits before those technologies become usable by CISC processors.

R2000 Processor Overview

The MIPS R2000 Processor consists of two tightly–coupled processors implemented on a single chip. The first processor is a full 32–bit RISC CPU. The second processor is a system control coprocessor (CP0), containing a TLB (Translation Lookaside Buffer) and control registers to support a virtual memory subsystem and separate caches for instructions and data. Figure 2.1 shows the functions incorporated within the R2000.

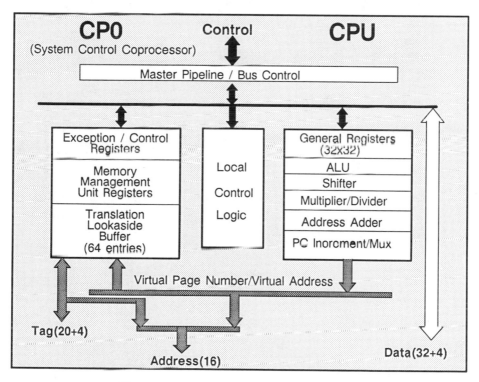

Figure 2.1   R2000 Functional Block Diagram

R2000 Processor Features

- **Full 32–bit Operation.** The R2000 contains thirty–two 32–bit registers, and all instructions and addresses are 32 bits.

- **Efficient Pipelining.** The CPU's 5–stage pipeline design assists in obtaining an execution rate approaching one instruction per cycle. Pipeline stalls and exceptional events are handled precisely and efficiently.

- **On–chip Cache Control.** The R2000 provides a high–bandwidth memory interface that handles separate external Instruction and Data caches ranging in size from 4 to 64 Kbytes each. Both caches are accessed during a single CPU cycle. All cache control logic is on chip.

- **On–chip Memory Management Unit.** a fully–associative, 64–entry Translation Lookaside Buffer (TLB) provides fast address translation for virtual–to–physical memory mapping of the 4–Gbyte virtual address space.

- **Coprocessor Interface.** the R2000 generates all addresses and handles memory interface control for up to three additional tightly–coupled external coprocessors.

R2000 CPU Registers

The R2000 CPU provides 32 general purpose 32–bit registers, a 32–bit Program Counter, and two 32–bit registers that hold the results of integer multiply and divide operations. The CPU registers are shown in Figure 2.2 and are described in detail later in this chapter. Note that there is no Program Status Word (PSW) register shown in this figure: the functions traditionally provided by a PSW register are instead provided in the *Status* and *Cause* registers incorporated within the System Control Coprocessor (CP0).

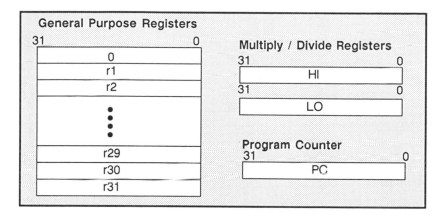

Figure 2.2 R2000 CPU Registers

Instruction Set Overview

All R2000 instructions are 32 bits long and there are only three instruction formats as shown in Figure 2.3. This approach simplifies instruction decoding. More complicated (and less frequently used) operations and addressing modes can be synthesized by the compiler using sequences of simple instructions.

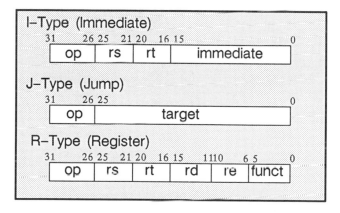

Figure 2.3 R2000 Instruction Formats

The R2000 instruction set can be divided into the following groups:

- **Load/Store** instructions move data between memory and general registers. They are all I–type instructions, since the only addressing mode supported is base register plus 16–bit, signed immediate offset.

- **Computational** instructions perform arithmetic, logical and shift operations on values in registers. They occur in both R–type (both operands and the result are registers) and I–type (one operand is a 16–bit immediate) formats.

- **Jump and Branch** instructions change the control flow of a program. Jumps are always to a paged absolute address formed by combining a 26–bit target with four bits of the Program Counter (J–type format, for subroutine calls) or 32–bit register addresses (R–type, for returns and dispatches). Branches have 16–bit offsets relative to the program counter (I–type). Jump and Link instructions save a return address in Register 31.

- **Coprocessor** instructions perform operations in the coprocessors. Coprocessor Loads and Stores are I–type. Coprocessor computational instructions have coprocessor–dependent formats (see the R2010 FPA instructions in **Chapter 7**).

- **Coprocessor 0** instructions perform operations on the System Control Coprocessor (CP0) registers to manipulate the memory management and exception handling facilities of the processor.

- **Special** instructions perform a variety of tasks, including movement of data between special and general registers, system calls, and breakpoint. They are always R–type.

Table 2.1 lists the instruction set of the R2000 Processor. A more detailed summary is provided in **Chapter 3** and a complete description of each instruction is contained in **Appendix A**.

OP	Description	OP	Description
	Load/Store Instructions		**Multiply/Divide Instructions**
LB	Load Byte	MULT	Multiply
LBU	Load Byte Unsigned	MULTU	Multiply Unsigned
LH	Load Halfword	DIV	Divide
LHU	Load Halfword Unsigned	DIVU	Divide Unsigned
LW	Load Word		
LWL	Load Word Left	MFHI	Move From HI
LWR	Load Word Right	MTHI	Move To HI
		MFLO	Move From LO
SB	Store Byte	MTLO	Move To LO
SH	Store Halfword		**Jump and Branch Instructions**
SW	Store Word		
SWL	Store Word Left	J	Jump
SWR	Store Word Right	JAL	Jump And Link
	Arithmetic Instructions (ALU Immediate)	JR	Jump to Register
		JALR	Jump And Link Register
ADDI	Add Immediate	BEQ	Branch on Equal
ADDIU	Add Immediate Unsigned	BNE	Branch on Not Equal
SLTI	Set on Less Than Immediate	BLEZ	Branch on Less than or Equal to Zero
SLTIU	Set on Less Than Immediate Unsigned	BGTZ	Branch on Greater Than Zero
		BLTZ	Branch on Less Than Zero
ANDI	AND Immediate	BGEZ	Branch on Greater than or Equal to Zero
ORI	OR Immediate		
XORI	Exclusive OR Immediate	BLTZAL	Branch on Less Than Zero And Link
LUI	Load Upper Immediate	BGEZAL	Branch on Greater than or Equal to Zero And Link
	Arithmetic Instructions (3-operand, register-type)		**Coprocessor Instructions**
ADD	Add	LWCz	Load Word from Coprocessor
ADDU	Add Unsigned	SWCz	Store Word to Coprocessor
SUB	Subtract	MTCz	Move To Coprocessor
SUBU	Subtract Unsigned	MFCz	Move From Coprocessor
SLT	Set on Less Than	CTCz	Move Control to Coprocessor
SLTU	Set on Less Than Unsigned	CFCz	Move Control From Coprocessor
AND	AND	COPz	Coprocessor Operation
OR	OR	BCzT	Branch on Coprocessor z True
XOR	Exclusive OR	BCzF	Branch on Coprocessor z False
NOR	NOR		
	Shift Instructions		**System Control Coprocessor (CP0) Instructions**
SLL	Shift Left Logical		
SRL	Shift Right Logical	MTC0	Move To CP0
SRA	Shift Right Arithmetic	MFC0	Move From CP0
SLLV	Shift Left Logical Variable		
SRLV	Shift Right Logical Variable	TLBR	Read indexed TLB entry
SRAV	Shift Right Arithmetic Variable	TLBWI	Write Indexed TLB entry
	Special Instructions	TLBWR	Write Random TLB entry
		TLDP	Probe TLB for matching entry
SYSCALL	System Call	RFE	Restore From Exception
BREAK	Break		

Table 2.1 R2000 Instruction Summary

R2000 Processor Programming Model

This section describes organization of data in registers and in memory and the set of general registers available. It also gives a summary description of all the R2000 CPU registers.

Data Formats and Addressing

The R2000 defines a 32–bit word, a 16–bit half word and an 8–bit byte. The byte ordering is configurable (configuration occurs during hardware reset) into either *big–endian* or *little–endian* byte ordering:

- When configured as a **big–endian** system, byte 0 is always the most significant (leftmost) byte, thereby providing compatibility with MC 68000® and IBM 370® conventions.

- When configured as a **little–endian** system, byte 0 is always the least significant (rightmost) byte, which is compatible with iAPX® x86, NS 32000®, and DEC VAX® conventions.

For purposes of exposition, bit 0 is always the least significant (rightmost) bit; thus bit designations are always little–endian (although no instructions explicitly designate bit positions within words).

Figures 2.4 and 2.5 show the ordering of bytes within words and the ordering of words within multiple–word structures for the big–endian and little–endian conventions.

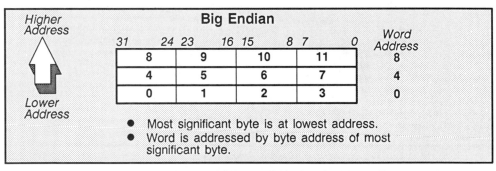

Figure 2.4 Addresses of Bytes within Words: Big Endian

Little Endian

Higher Address	31 24	23 16	15 8	7 0	Word Address
	11	10	9	8	8
	7	6	5	4	4
	3	2	1	0	0

Lower Address

- Least significant byte is at lowest address.
- Word is addressed by byte address of least significant byte.

Figure 2.5 Addresses of Bytes within Words: Little Endian

The R2000 uses byte addressing, with alignment constraints, for half word and word accesses; half word accesses must be aligned on an even byte boundary and word accesses must be aligned on a byte boundary divisible by four.

As shown in Figures 2.4 and 2.5, the address of a multiple–byte data item is the address of the most–significant byte on a big–endian configuration, and is the address of the least–significant byte on a little–endian configuration.

Special instructions are provided for addressing words that are not aligned on 4–byte (word) boundaries (Load/Store–Word–Left/Right; LWL, LWR, SWL, SWR). These instructions are used in pairs to provide addressing of misaligned words with one additional instruction cycle over that required for aligned words. Figure 2.6 shows the bytes accessed when addressing a misaligned word with a byte address of 3 for each of the two conventions.

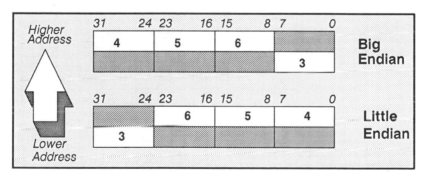

Figure 2.6 Misaligned Word: Byte Addresses

R2000 CPU General Registers

Figure 2.7 shows the R2000 CPU registers. There are 32 general registers, each consisting of a single word (32 bits). The 32 general registers are treated symmetrically, with two exceptions: *r0* is hardwired to a zero value, and *r31* is the link register for Jump And Link instructions.

Register *r0* may be specified as a target register for any instruction when the result of the operation is discarded. The register maintains a value of zero under all conditions when used as a source register.

The two Multiply/Divide registers (HI, LO) store the double–word, 64–bit result of multiply operations and the quotient and remainder of divide operations.

NOTE: In addition to the CPU's general registers, the system control coprocessor (CP0) has a number of special purpose registers that are used in conjunction with the memory management system and during exception processing. Refer to **Chapter 4** for a description of the memory management registers and to **Chapter 5** for a discussion of the exception handling registers.

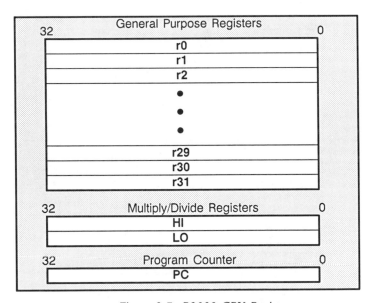

Figure 2.7 R2000 CPU Registers

R2000 System Control Coprocessor (CP0)

The R2000 can operate with up to four tightly–coupled coprocessors (designated CP0 through CP3). The System Control Coprocessor (or CP0), is incorporated on the R2000 chip and supports the virtual memory system and exception handling functions of the R2000. The virtual memory system is implemented using a Translation Lookaside Buffer and a group of programmable registers as shown in Figure 2.8.

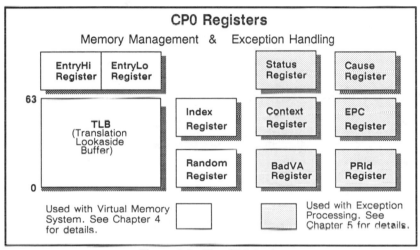

Figure 2.8 The CP0 Registers

System Control Coprocessor (CP0) Registers

The CP0 registers shown in Figure 2.8 are used to manipulate the memory management and exception handling capabilities of the R2000. Table 2.2 provides a brief description of each register. Refer to **Chapter 4** for a detailed description of the registers associated with the virtual memory system and refer to **Chapter 5** for descriptions of the exception processing registers.

Register	Description
EntryHi	High half of a TLB entry
EntryLo	Low half of a TLB entry
Index	Programmable pointer into TLB array
Random	Pseudo-random pointer into TLB array
Status	Mode, interrupt enables, and diagnostic status info
Cause	Indicates nature of last exception
EPC	Exception Program Counter
Context	Pointer into kernel's virtual Page Table Entry array
BadVA	Most recent bad virtual address
PRId	Processor revision identification

Table 2.2   System Control Coprocessor (CP0) Registers

Memory Management System

The R2000 has an addressing range of 4 Gbytes. However, since most R2000 systems implement a physical memory smaller than 4 Gbytes, the R2000 provides for the logical expansion of memory space by translating addresses composed in a large virtual address space into available physical memory addresses. The 4 GByte address space is divided into 2 Gbytes for users and 2 GBytes for the kernel.

The TLB (Translation Lookaside Buffer)

Virtual memory mapping is assisted by the Translation Lookaside Buffer (TLB). The on-chip TLB provides very fast virtual memory access and is well-matched to the requirements of multi-tasking operating systems. The fully-associative TLB contains 64 entries, each of which maps a 4-Kbyte page, with controls for read/write access, cacheability, and process identification. The TLB allows each user to access up to 2 Gbytes of virtual address space.

R2000 Operating Modes

The R2000 has two operating modes: *User* mode and *Kernel* mode. The R2000 normally operates in the User mode until an exception is detected forcing it into the Kernel mode. It remains in the Kernel mode until a Restore From Exception *(RFE)* instruction is executed. The manner in which memory addresses are translated or *mapped* depends on the operating mode of the R2000. Figure 2.9 shows the virtual address space for the two operating modes.

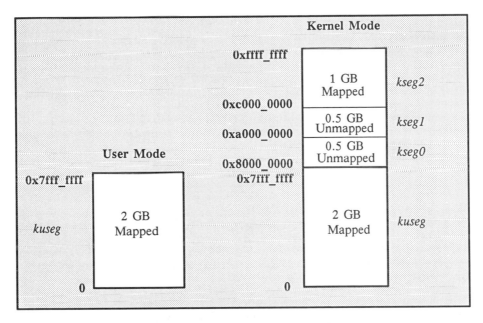

Figure 2.9 R2000 Virtual Addressing

User Mode. In this mode, a single, uniform virtual address space (kuseg) of 2 Gbyte is available. Each virtual address is extended with a 6 bit process identifier field to form unique virtual addresses for up to 64 user processes. All references to this segment are mapped through the TLB. Use of the cache is determined by bit settings for each page within the TLB entries.

Kernel Mode. Four separate segments are defined in this mode:

- *kuseg.* When in the Kernel mode, references to this segment are treated just like User mode references, thus streamlining kernel access to user data.

- *kseg0.* References to this 512–Mbyte segment use cache memory but are not mapped through the TLB. Instead, they always map to the first 0.5 GBytes of physical memory.

- *kseg1.* References to this 512–Mbyte segment are not mapped through the TLB and do not use the cache. Instead, they are hard–mapped into the same 0.5–GByte segment of physical memory space as *kseg0.*

- *kseg2.* References to this 1–Gbyte segment are always mapped through the TLB, and use of the cache is determined by bit settings within the TLB entries.

R2000 Pipeline Architecture

The execution of a single R2000 instruction consists of five primary steps:

1) **IF**—Fetch the instruction (I-Cache).
2) **RD**—Read any required operands from CPU registers while decoding the instruction.
3) **ALU**—Perform the required operation on instruction operands.
4) **MEM**—Access memory (D-Cache).
5) **WB**—Write back results to register file.

Each of these steps requires approximately one CPU cycle as shown in Figure 2.9 (parts of some operations lap over into another cycle while other operations require only 1/2 cycle).

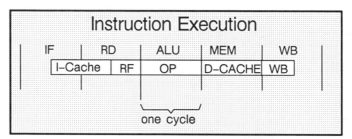

Figure 2.9 Instruction Execution Sequence

The R2000 uses a 5–stage pipeline to achieve an instruction execution rate approaching one instruction per CPU cycle. Thus, execution of five instructions at a time are overlapped as shown in Figure 2.10.

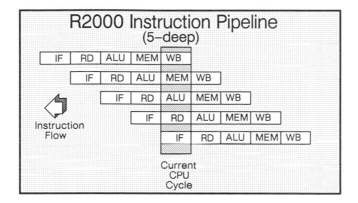

Figure 2.10   R2000 Instruction Pipeline

This pipeline operates efficiently because different CPU resources (address and data bus accesses, ALU operations, register accesses, and so on) are utilized on a non-interfering basis. Refer to **Chapter 3** for a detailed discussion of the instruction pipeline.

Memory System Hierarchy

The high performance capabilities of the R2000 Processor demand system configurations incorporating techniques frequently employed in large, mainframe computers but seldom encountered in systems based on more traditional microprocessors.

A primary goal of RISC machines is to achieve an instruction execution rate of one instruction per CPU cycle. The MIPS R2000 approaches this goal by means of a compact and uniform instruction set, a deep instruction pipeline (as described above), and careful adaptation to optimizing compilers. Many of the advantages obtained from these techniques can, however, be negated by an inefficient memory system.

Figure 2.11 illustrates memory in a simple microprocessor system. In this system, the CPU outputs addresses to memory and reads instructions and data from memory or writes data to memory. The memory space is completely undifferentiated: instructions, data, and I/O devices are all treated the same. In such a system, a primary limiting performance factor is memory bandwidth.

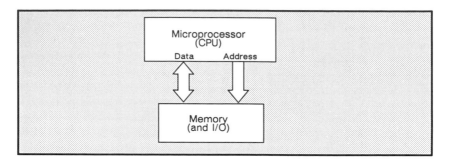

Figure 2.11 A Simple Microprocessor Memory System

Figure 2.12 illustrates a memory system that supports the significantly greater memory bandwidth required to take full advantage of the R2000's performance capabilities. The key features of this system are:

- **External Cache Memory**. Local, high–speed memory (called *cache* memory) is used to hold instructions and data that is repetitively accessed by the CPU (for example, within a program loop) and thus reduces the number of references that must be made to the slower speed main memory. Some microprocessors provide a limited amount of cache memory on the CPU chip itself. The external caches supported by the R2000 can be much larger; while a small cache can improve performance of some programs, significant improvements for a wide range of programs require large caches.

- **Separate Caches for Data and Instructions**. Even with high–speed caches, memory speed can still be a limiting factor because of the fast cycle time of a high–performance microprocessor. The R2000 supports separate caches for instructions and data and alternates accesses of the two caches during each CPU cycle. Thus, the processor can obtain data and instructions at the cycle rate of the CPU using caches constructed with commercially available static RAM devices.

- **Write Buffer**. In order to ensure data consistency, all data that is written to the data cache must also be written out to main memory. To relieve the CPU of this responsibility (and the inherent performance burden) the R2000 supports an interface to a write buffer. The R2020 Write Buffer captures data and addresses output by the CPU and ensures that the data is passed on to main memory.

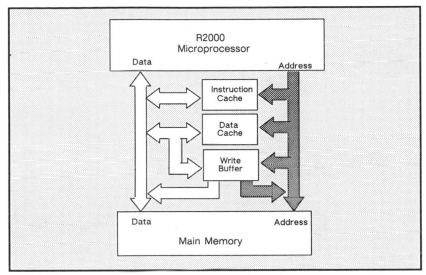

Figure 2.12   An R2000 System with a High–Performance Memory System

R2000 Instruction Set Summary

This chapter provides an overview of the R2000 instruction set by presenting each category of instructions in a tabular summary form. It also provides a detailed discussion of the instruction pipeline. Refer to **Appendix A** for a detailed description of each instruction.

Instruction Formats

Every R2000 instruction consists of a single word (32 bits) aligned on a word boundary. There are only three instruction formats as shown in Figure 3.1. This approach simplifies instruction decoding. More complicated (and less frequently used) operations and addressing modes can be synthesized by the compiler.

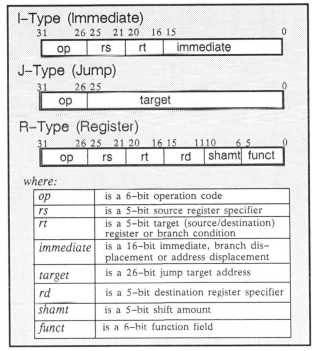

Figure 3.1 R2000 Instruction Formats

Instruction Notational Conventions

In this manual, all variable sub-fields in an instruction format (such as *rs, rt, immediate*, and so on) are shown in lower-case names.

For the sake of clarity, an alias is sometimes used for a variable sub-field in the formats of specific instructions. For example, *rs = base* in the format for Load and Store instructions. Such an alias is always lower case, since it refers to a variable sub-field.

Instruction opcodes are shown in all upper case.

The actual bit encoding for all the mnemonics is specified at the end of **Appendix A**.

Load and Store Instructions

Load/Store instructions move data between memory and general registers. They are all I-type instructions. The only addressing mode directly supported is base register plus 16-bit signed immediate offset.

All load operations have a latency of one instruction. That is, the data being loaded from memory into a register is not available to the instruction that immediately follows the load instruction: the data is available to the second instruction after the load instruction. An exception is the target register for the "load word left" and "load word right" instructions, which may be specified as the same register used as the destination of a load instruction that immediately precedes it. (Refer to **R2000 Instruction Pipeline** at the end of this chapter for a detailed discussion of load instruction latency.)

The Load/Store instruction opcode determines the access type which indicates the size of the data item to be loaded or stored as shown in Table 3.2. Regardless of access type or byte-numbering order (endian-ness), the address specifies the byte which has the smallest byte address of all the bytes in the addressed field. For a big-endian machine, this is the most significant byte; for a little-endian machine, this is the least significant byte.

The bytes within the addressed word that are used can be determined directly from the access type and the two low-order bits of the address, as shown in Table 3.2. Note that certain combinations of access type and low-order address bits can never occur: only the combinations shown in Table 3.2 are permissible.

Access Type 1 0	Low-Order Address Bits 1 0	Bytes Accessed							
		Big-Endian 31 ——————— 0				Little-Endian 31 ——————— 0			
1 1 (word)	0 0	0	1	2	3	3	2	1	0
1 0 (triple-byte)	0 0	0	1	2			2	1	0
	0 1		1	2	3	3	2	1	
0 1 (halfword)	0 0	0	1					1	0
	1 0			2	3	3	2		
0 0 (byte)	0 0	0							0
	0 1		1					1	
	1 0			2			2		
	1 1				3	3			

Table 3.2 Byte Specifications for Loads/Stores

Table 3.3 summarizes the R2000 Load and Store instructions.

Instruction	Format and Description	op	base	rt	offset
Load Byte	LB rt,offset(base) Sign-extend 16-bit offset and add to contents of register base to form address. Sign-extend contents of addressed byte and load into rt.				
Load Byte Unsigned	LBU rt,offset(base) Sign-extend 16-bit offset and add to contents of register base to form address. Zero –extend contents of addressed byte and load into rt.				
Load Halfword	LH rt,offset(base) Sign-extend 16-bit offset and add to contents of register base to form address. Sign-extend contents of addressed halfword and load into rt.				
Load Halfword Unsigned	LHU rt,offset(base) Sign-extend 16-bit offset and add to contents of register base to form address. Zero –extend contents of addressed halfword and load into rt.				
Load Word	LW rt,offset(base) Sign-extend 16-bit offset and add to contents of register base to form address. Load contents of addressed word into register rt.				
Load Word Left	LWL rt,offset(base) Sign-extend 16-bit offset and add to contents of register base to form address. Shift addressed word left so that addressed byte is leftmost byte of a word. Merge bytes from memory with contents of register rt and load result into register rt.				
Load Word Right	LWR rt,offset(base) Sign-extend 16-bit offset and add to contents of register base to form address. Shift addressed word right so that addressed byte is rightmost byte of a word. Merge bytes from memory with contents of register rt and load result into register rt.				
Store Byte	SB rt,offset(base) Sign-extend 16-bit offset and add to contents of register base to form address. Store least significant byte of register rt at addressed location.				
Store Halfword	SH rt,offset(base) Sign-extend 16-bit offset and add to contents of register base to form address. Store least significant halfword of register rt at addressed location.				
Store Word	SW rt,offset(base) Sign-extend 16-bit offset and add to contents of register base to form address. Store least significant word of register rt at addressed location.				
Store Word Left	SWL rt,offset(base) Sign-extend 16-bit offset and add to contents of register base to form address. Shift contents of register rt left so that leftmost byte of the word is in position of addressed byte. Store bytes containing original data into corresponding bytes at addressed byte.				
Store Word Right	SWR rt,offset(base) Sign-extend 16-bit offset and add to contents of register base to form address. Shift contents of register rt right so that leftmost byte of the word is in position of addressed byte. Store bytes containing original data into corresponding bytes at addressed byte.				

Table 3.3 Load and Store Instruction Summary

Computational Instructions

Computational instructions perform arithmetic, logical and shift operations on values in registers. They occur in both R–type (both operands are registers) and I–type (one operand is a 16–bit immediate) formats. There are four categories of computational instructions:

- **ALU Immediate** instructions are summarized in Table 3.4a.

- **3–Operand Register–Type** instructions are summarized in Table 3.4b.

- **Shift** instructions are summarized in Table 3.4c.

- **Multiply/Divide** instructions are summarized in Table 3.4d.

Instruction	Format and Description
	op | rs | rt | immediate
ADD Immediate	*ADDI rt,rs,immediate* Add 16–bit sign–extended *immediate* to register *rs* and place 32–bit result in register *rt*. Trap on two's complement overflow.
ADD Immediate Unsigned	*ADDIU rt,rs,immediate* Add 16–bit sign–extended *immediate* to register *rs* and place 32–bit result in register *rt*. Do not trap on overflow.
Set on Less Than Immediate	*SLTI rt,rs,immediate* Compare 16–bit sign–extended *immediate* with register *rs* as signed 32–bit integers. Result = 1 if *rs* is less than *immediate;* otherwise result = 0. Place result in register *rt*.
Set on Less Than Unsigned Immediate	*SLTIU rt,rs,immediate* Compare 16–bit sign–extended *immediate* with register *rs* as unsigned 32–bit integers. Result = 1 if *rs* is less than *immediate;* otherwise result = 0. Place result in register *rt*.
AND Immediate	*ANDI rt,rs,immediate* Zero–extend 16–bit *immediate*, AND with contents of register *rs* and place result in register *rt*.
OR Immediate	*ORI rt,rs,immediate* Zero–extend 16–bit *immediate*, OR with contents of register *rs* and place result in register *rt*.
Exclusive OR Immediate	*XORI rt,rs,immediate* Zero–extend 16–bit *immediate*, exclusive OR with contents of register *rs* and place result in register *rt*.
Load Upper Immediate	*LUI rt,immediate* Shift 16–bit *immediate* left 16 bits. Set least significant 16 bits of word to zeroes. Store result in register *rt*.

Table 3.4a ALU Immediate Instruction Summary

Instruction	Format and Description	op	rs	rt	rd	ALUfunct
Add	*ADD rd,rs,rt* Add contents of registers *rs* and *rt* and place 32–bit result in register *rd*. Trap on two's complement overflow.
Add Unsigned	*ADDU rd,rs,rt* Add contents of registers *rs* and *rt* and place 32–bit result in register *rd*. Do not trap on overflow.
Subtract	*SUB rd,rs,rt* Subtract contents of registers *rt* from *rs* and place 32–bit result in register *rd*. Trap on two's complement overflow.
Subtract Unsigned	*SUBU rd,rs,rt* Subtract contents of registers *rt* from *rs* and place 32–bit result in register *rd*. Do not trap on overflow.
Set on Less Than	*SLT rd,rs,rt* Compare contents of register *rt* to register *rs* (as signed 32–bit integers). If register *rs* is less than *rt*, result = 1; otherwise, result = 0.
Set on Less Than Unsigned	*SLTU rd,rs,rt* Compare contents of register *rt* to register *rs* (as unsigned 32–bit integers). If register *rs* is less than *rt*, result = 1; otherwise, result = 0.
AND	*AND rd,rs,rt* Bitwise AND contents of registers *rs* and *rt* and place result in register *rd*.
OR	*OR rd,rs,rt* Bitwise OR contents of registers *rs* and *rt* and place result in register *rd*.
Exclusive OR	*XOR rd,rs,rt* Bitwise exclusive OR contents of registers *rs* and *rt* and place result in register *rd*.
NOR	*NOR rd,rs,rt* Bitwise NOR contents of registers *rs* and *rt* and place result in register *rd*.

Table 3.4b 3–Operand Register–Type Instruction Summary

Instruction	Format and Description
Shift Left Logical	*SLL rd,rt,shamt* Shift contents of register *rt* left by *shamt* bits, inserting zeroes into low order bits. Place 32–bit result in register *rd*.
Shift Right Logical	*SRL rd,rt,shamt* Shift contents of register *rt* right by *shamt* bits, inserting zeroes into high order bits. Place 32–bit result in register *rd*.
Shift Right Arithmetic	*SRA rd,rt,shamt* Shift contents of register *rt* right by *shamt* bits, sign–extending the high order bits. Place 32–bit result in register *rd*.
Shift Left Logical Variable	*SLLV rd,rt,rs* Shift contents of register *rt* left. Low–order 5 bits of register *rs* specify number of bits to shift. Insert zeroes into low order bits of *rt* and place 32–bit result in register *rd*.
Shift Right Logical Variable	*SRLV rd,rt,rs* Shift contents of register *rt* right. Low–order 5 bits of register *rs* specify number of bits to shift. Insert zeroes into high order bits of *rt* and place 32–bit result in register *rd*.
Shift Right Arithmetic Variable	*SRAV rd,rt,rs* Shift contents of register *rt* right. Low–order 5 bits of register *rs* specify number of bits to shift. Sign–extend the high order bits of *rt* and place 32–bit result in register *rd*.

Table 3.4c Shift Instruction Summary

Instruction	Format and Description
Multiply	MULT rs,rt Multiply contents of registers rs and rt as twos complement values. Place 64-bit result in special registers HI / LO.
Multiply Unsigned	MULTU rs,rt Multiply contents of registers rs and rt as unsigned values. Place 64-bit result in special registers HI / LO.
Divide	DIV rs,rt Divide contents of register rs by rt treating operands as twos complements values. Place 32-bit quotient in special register LO, and 32-bit remainder in HI.
Divide Unsigned	DIVU rs,rt Divide contents of register rs by rt treating operands as unsigned values. Place the 32-bit quotient in special register LO, and the 32-bit remainder in HI.
Move From HI	MFHI rd Move contents of special register HI to register rd.
Move From LO	MFLO rd Move contents of special register LO to register rd.
Move To HI	MTHI rd Move contents of register rd to special register HI.
Move To LO	MTLO rd Move contents of register rd to special register LO.

Table 3.4d Multiply/Divide Instruction Summary

Jump and Branch Instructions

Jump and Branch instructions change the control flow of a program. All Jump and Branch instructions occur with a one instruction delay: that is, the instruction immediately following the jump or branch is always executed while the target instruction is being fetched from storage. Refer to **The Delayed Instruction Slot** at the end of this chapter for a detailed discussion of the delayed Dump and Branch instructions.

The J-type instruction format is used for both jumps and jump-and-links for subroutine calls. In this format, the 26-bit target address is shifted left two bits, and combined with the high-order 4 bits of the current program counter to form a 32-bit absolute address.

The R-type instruction format which takes a 32-bit byte address contained in a register is used for returns, dispatches, and cross-page jumps.

Branches have 16-bit offsets relative to the program counter (I-type). Jump-and-Link and Branch-and-Link instructions save a return address in Register 31.

Table 3.5a summarizes the R2000 Jump instructions and Table 3.5b summarizes the Branch instructions.

Instruction	Format and Description
Jump	*J target* Shift 26 bit target address left two bits, combine with high-order 4 bits of PC and jump to address with a one instruction delay.
Jump And Lind	*JAL target* Shift 26-bit target address left two bits, combine with high-order 4 bits of PC and jump to address with a one instruction delay. Place address of instruction following delay slot in r31 (link register).
Jump Register	*JR rs* Jump to address contained in register *rs* with a one instruction delay.
Jump And Link Register	*JALR rs, rd* Jump to address contained in register *rs* with a one instruction delay. Place address of instruction following delay slot in *rd*.

Table 3.5a Jump Instruction Summary

Instruction	Format and Description
	Branch Target: All Branch instruction target addresses are computed as follows: Add address of instruction in delay slot and the 16-bit *offset* (shifted left two bits and sign-extended to 32 bits). All branches occur with a delay of one instruction.
Branch on Equal	*BEQ rs,rt,offset* Branch to target address if register *rs* = *rt*.
Branch on Not Equal	*BNE rs,rt,offset* Branch to target address if register *rs* ≠ *rt*.
Branch on Less than or Equal Zero	*BLEZ rs,offset* Branch to target address if register *rs* less than or = 0.
Branch on Greater Than Zero	*BGTZ rs,offset* Branch to target address if register *rs* greater than 0.
Branch on Less Than Zero	*BLTZ rs,offset* Branch to target address if register *rs* less than 0.
Branch on Greater than or Equal Zero	*BGEZ rs,offset* Branch to target address if register *rs* greater than or = to 0.
Branch on Less Than Zero And Link	*BLTZAL rs,offset* Place address of instruction following delay slot in register r31 (link register). Branch to target address if register *rs* less than 0.
Branch on Greater than or Equal Zero And Link	*BGEZAL rs,offset* Place address of instruction following delay slot in register r31 (link register). Branch to target address if register *rs* is greater than or = to 0.

Table 3.5b Branch Instruction Summary

Special Instructions

The two **Special** instructions let software initiate traps. They are always R-type. Table 3.6 summarizes the Special instructions.

Instruction	Format and Description
System Call	*SYSCALL* Initiates system call trap, immediately transferring control to exception handler.
Breakpoint	*BREAK* Initiates breakpoint trap, immediately transferring control to exception handler.

Table 3.6 Special Instructions

Coprocessor Instructions

Coprocessor instructions perform operations in the coprocessors. Coprocessor Loads and Stores are I-type. Coprocessor computational instructions have coprocessor-dependent formats (see coprocessor manuals). Table 3.7 summarizes the Coprocessor instructions.

Instruction	Format and Description
Load Word to Coprocessor	*LWCz rt,offset(base)* Sign-extend 16-bit *offset* and add to *base* to form address. Load contents of addressed word into coprocessor register *rt* of coprocessor unit z.
Store Word from Coprocessor	*SWCz rt,offset(base)* Sign-extend 16-bit *offset* and add to *base* to form address. Store contents of coprocessor register *rt* from coprocessor unit z at addressed memory word.
Move To Coprocessor	*MTCz rt,rd* Move contents of CPU register *rt* into coprocessor register *rd* of coprocessor unit z.
Move From Coprocessor	*MFCz rt,rd* Move contents of coprocessor register *rd* from coprocessor unit z to CPU register *rt*.
Move Control To Coprocessor	*CTCz rt,rd* Move contents of CPU register *rt* into coprocessor control register *rd* of coprocessor unit z.
Move Control From Coprocessor	*CFCz rt,rd* Move contents of control register *rd* of coprocessor unit z into CPU register *rt*.
Coprocessor Operation	*COPz cofun* Coprocessor z performs an operation. The state of the R2000 is not modified by a coprocessor operation.
Branch on Coprocessor z True	*BCzT offset* Compute a branch target address by adding address of instruction in the 16-bit *offset* (shifted left two bits and sign-extended to 32 bits). Branch to the target address (with a delay of one instruction) if coprocessor z's condition line is true.
Branch on Coprocessor z False	*BCzF offset* Compute a branch target address by adding address of instruction in the 16-bit *offset* (shifted left two bits and sign-extended to 32 bits). Branch to the target address (with a delay of one instruction) if coprocessor z's condition line is false.

Table 3.7 R2000 Coprocessor Instruction Summary

System Control Coprocessor (CP0) Instructions

Coprocessor 0 instructions perform operations on the System Control Coprocessor (CP0) registers to manipulate the memory management and exception handling facilities of the processor. Table 3.8 summarizes the instructions available to work with CP0.

Instruction	Format and Description
Move To CP0	*MTC0 rt,rd* Load contents of CPU register *rt* into register *rd* of CP0.
Move From CP0	*MFC0 rt,rd* Load contents of CP0 register *rd* into CPU register *rt*.
Read Indexed TLB Entry	*TLBR* Load *EntryHi* and *EntryLo* registers with TLB entry pointed at by *Index* register.
Write Indexed TLB Entry	*TLBWI* Load TLB entry pointed at by *Index* register with contents of *EntryHi* and *EntryLo* registers.
Write Random TLB Entry	*TLBWR* Load TLB entry pointed at by *Random* register with contents of *EntryHi* and *EntryLo* registers.
Probe TLB for Matching Entry	*TLBP* Load *Index* register with address of TLB entry whose contents match *EntryHi* and *EntryLo*. If no TLB entry matches, set high–order bit of *Index* register.
Restore From Exception	*RFE* Restore previous interrupt mask and mode bits of *Status* register into current status bits. Restore old status bits into previous status bits.

Table 3.8 System Control Coprocessor (CP0) Instruction Summary

R2000 Instruction Pipeline

The execution of a single instruction consists of five primary steps or *pipe stages*:

1) **IF**—Instruction Fetch. Access the TLB and calculate the instruction address required to read an instruction from the I–Cache. Note that the instruction is not actually read into the processor until the beginning (phase 1) of the RD pipe stage.

2) **RD**—Read any required operands from CPU registers (RF = Register Fetch) while decoding the instruction.

3) **ALU**—Perform the required operation on instruction operands.

4) **MEM**—Access memory (D–Cache) if required (for a Load or Store instruction).

5) **WB**—Write back ALU results or value loaded from D–cache to register file.

Each of these steps requires approximately one CPU cycle as shown in Figure 3.2 (parts of some operations lap over into another cycle while other operations require only 1/2 cycle).

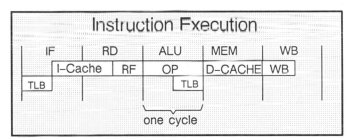

Figure 3.2 Instruction Execution Sequence

To achieve an instruction execution rate approaching one instruction per CPU cycle, a five–instruction pipeline is utilized. Thus, five instructions at a time are executed in an overlapped fashion as shown in Figure 3.3.

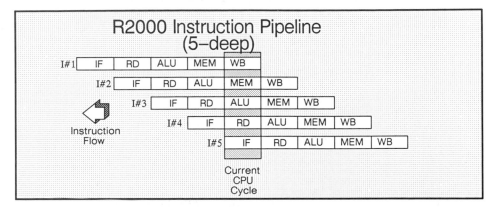

Figure 3.3 R2000 Instruction Pipeline

The Delayed Instruction Slot

The R2000 uses a number of techniques internally to enable execution of all instructions in a single cycle; however, there are two categories of instructions whose special requirements could disturb the smooth flow of instructions through the pipeline.

- Load instructions have a delay, or latency, of one cycle before the data being loaded is available to another instruction.

- Jump and Branch instructions also have a delay of one cycle while they fetch the instruction and the target address if the branch is taken.

One technique for dealing with the delay inherent with these instructions would be to stall the flow of instructions through the pipeline whenever a load, jump, or branch is executed. However, in addition to the negative impact that this technique would have on instruction throughput, it would also complicate the pipeline logic, exception processing, and system synchronization.

The technique used in the R2000 is to continue execution despite the delay. Loads, jumps, and branches do not interrupt the normal flow of instructions through the pipeline; *the processor always executes the instruction immediately following one of these "delayed" instructions.* Instead of having the processor deal with pipeline delays, the R2000 turns over the responsibility for dealing with delayed instructions to software. Thus, an assembler can insert an appropriate instruction immediately following a delayed instruction and has the responsibility of ensuring that the inserted instruction will not be affected by the delay.

Delayed Loads

Figure 3.4 shows three instructions in the R2000 pipeline. Instruction 1 (I#1) is a Load instruction. The data from the load is not available until the end of the I#1 MEM cycle – too late to be used by I#2 during its ALU cycle, but available to I#3 for its ALU cycle. Therefore, software must ensure that I#2 does not depend on data loaded by I#1. Usually, a compiler can reorganize instructions so that something useful is executed during the delay slot or, if no other instruction is available, can insert a NOP (no operation) instruction in the slot.

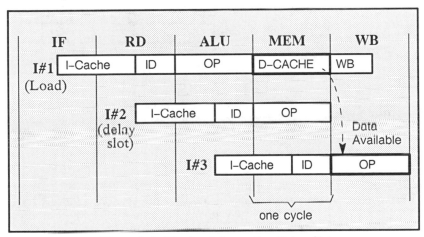

Figure 3.4 The Load Instruction Delay Slot

Delayed Jumps and Branches

Figure 3.5 also shows three instructions in the R2000 pipeline. Instruction 1 (I#1) in this case is a Branch instruction. I#1 must calculate a branch target address, and that address is not available until the beginning of the ALU cycle of I#1 — too late for the I–Cache access of I#2 but available to I#3 for its I–Cache access. The instruction in the delay slot (I#2) will always be executed before the branch or jump actually occurs.

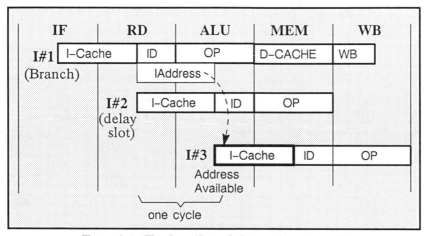

Figure 3.5 The Jump/Branch Instruction Delay Slot

An assembler has several possibilities for utilizing the branch delay slot productively:

- It can insert an instruction that logically precedes the branch instruction in the delay slot since the instruction immediately following the jump/branch effectively belongs to the block preceding the transfer instruction.

- It can replicate the instruction that is the target of the branch/jump into the delay slot provided that no side–effects occur if the branch falls through.

- It can move an instruction up from below the branch into the delay slot, provided that no side–effects occur if the branch is taken.

- If no other instruction is available, it can insert a NOP instruction in the delay slot.

4
Memory Management System

The R2000 provides a full-featured memory management unit (MMU) utilizing an on-chip Translation Lookaside Buffer (TLB) to provide very fast virtual memory accesses. This chapter describes the operation of the TLB and the CP0 registers that provide the software interface to the TLB. The memory mapping scheme supported by the R2000 to translate virtual addresses to physical addresses is also described in detail.

Memory System Architecture

The R2000's virtual memory system logically expands the CPU's physical memory space by translating addresses composed in a large virtual address space into the physical memory space of the R2000.

Figure 4.1 shows the form of an R2000 virtual address. The most significant 20 bits of a 32-bit virtual address are called the virtual page number, or VPN. The VPN allows mapping of 4 Kbyte pages, while the least significant 12 bits (the offset within a page) are passed along unchanged to form the physical address. The three most significant bits of VPN (bits 31..29) further define how addresses are mapped according to whether the R2000 is in user mode or kernel mode (these modes are described in the paragraphs that follow).

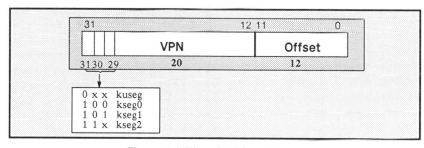

Figure 4.1 Virtual Address Format

A 6-bit process identifier field is appended to each virtual address to form unique virtual addresses for up to 64 processes. The mapping of these extended, process-unique virtual addresses to physical addresses need not be one-to-one; virtual addresses of two or more different processes may map to the same physical address.

Privilege States

The R2000 provides two privilege states: the Kernel mode, which is analogous to the "supervisory" mode provided by many machines, and the User mode, where non-supervisory programs are executed. The R2000 enters the Kernel mode whenever an exception is detected and remains in the Kernel mode until a Restore From Exception (*rfe*) instruction is executed.

Address mapping is different for Kernel and User modes. To simplify the management of user state from within the Kernel, the user–mode address space is a subset of the Kernel–mode address space. Figure 4.2 shows the virtual–to–physical memory map for both the User mode and Kernel mode segments.

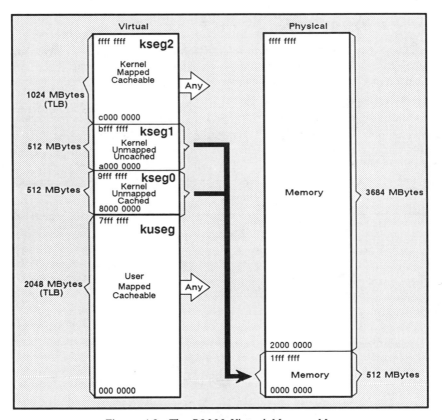

Figure 4.2 The R2000 Virtual Memory Map

User-Mode Virtual Addressing

When the processor is operating in User mode, a single, uniform virtual address space (**kuseg**) of 2 Gbytes is available for users. All valid User-mode virtual addresses have the most-significant bit cleared to 0. An attempt to reference an address with the most-significant bit set while in the User mode causes an Address Error exception. (See **Chapter 5**.)

The 2 Gbyte User segment starts at address zero. The TLB maps all references to kuseg identically from Kernel and User modes and controls access cacheability. (The *N* bit in a TLB entry determines whether the reference will be cached.)

Kuseg is typically used to hold user code and data, and the current user process typically resides in kuseg.

Kernel-Mode Virtual Addressing

When the processor is operating in Kernel mode, three distinct virtual address spaces (in addition to **kuseg**) are simultaneously available. The three segments dedicated to the kernel are:

- **kseg0**. This cached, unmapped segment starts at virtual address 0x8000_0000 and is 512 Mbytes long.

- **kseg1**. This uncached, unmapped segment begins at virtual address 0xa000_0000 and is 512 Mbytes long.

- **kseg2**. This kernel-mapped, cacheable segment begins at virtual address 0xc000_0000 and is 1 Gbytes long.

Kseg0. When the most-significant three bits of the virtual address are "100," the virtual address space selected is a 512-Mbyte kernel physical space (kseg0). The R2000 direct-maps references within kseg0 onto the first 512 Mbytes of physical address space. These references use cache memory, but they do not use TLB entries. Thus, kseg0 is typically used for kernel executable code and some kernel data.

Kseg1. When the most-significant three bits of the virtual address are "101," the virtual address space selected is a 512-Mbyte kernel physical space (kseg1). The processor directly maps kseg1 onto the first 512 Mbytes of physical space and uses no TLB entries. Unlike kseg0, kseg1 uses uncached references. An operating system typically uses kseg1 for I/O registers, ROM code, and disk buffers.

Kseg2. When the most–significant two bits of the virtual address are "11," the virtual address space selected is a 1024 Mbyte kernel virtual space (kseg2). Like kuseg, kseg2 uses TLB entries to map virtual addresses to arbitrary physical ones, with or without caching. (The *N* bit in a TLB entry determines whether the reference will be cached.) An operating system typically uses kseg2 for stacks and per-process data that it must remap on context switches, for user page tables (memory map), and for some dynamically allocated data areas. Kseg2 allows selective caching and mapping on a per–page basis, rather than requiring an all or nothing approach.

Virtual Memory and the TLB

Mapped virtual addresses are translated into physical addresses using a Translation Lookaside Buffer (TLB). The TLB is a fully associative memory device that holds 64 entries to provide mapping of 64 4Kbyte pages. When address mapping is indicated (that is, when the access is in *kuseg* or *kseg2*), each TLB entry is simultaneously checked for a match with the extended virtual address.

The CPU supports up to four coprocessors. Coprocessor 0 (CP0), which is called the System Control Coprocessor, is implemented as an integral part of the R2000. CP0 supports address translation, exception handling, and other "privileged" operations. It consists of the 64-entry TLB plus the ten registers shown in Figure 4.3. The sections that follow describe how each of the four TLB–related registers is used. (Note: CP0 functions and registers associated with exception handling are described in **Chapter 5**.)

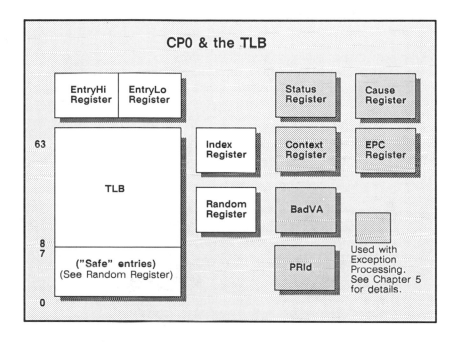

Figure 4.3 The CP0 Registers & the TLB.

TLB Entries

Each TLB entry is 64 bits wide and its format is shown in Figure 4.4. Each of the fields of a TLB entry has a corresponding field in the EntryHi/EntryLo register pair described next. Refer to Figure 4.5 for a description of each of the TLB entry fields.

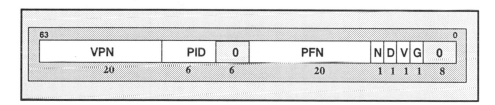

Figure 4.4 Format of a TLB Entry

EntryHi & EntryLo Registers

These two registers provide the data pathway through which the TLB is read, written, or probed. When address translation exceptions occur, these registers are loaded with relevant information about the address that caused the exception. The format of the *EntryHi* and *EntryLo* register pair a is the same as the format of TLB entry and is illustrated in Figure 4.5.

EntryLo is the natural form of a Page Table Entry (PTE); however, since PTEs are always loaded by system software, not by the R2000 hardware, an operating system can use another format for memory–resident PTEs.

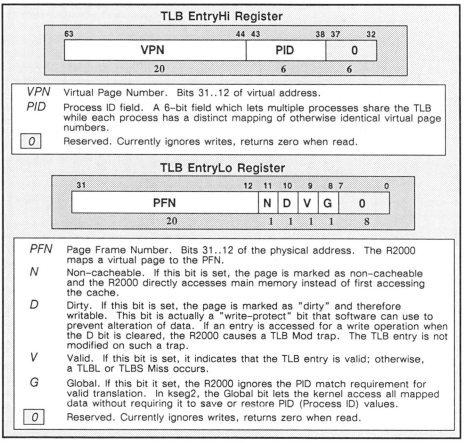

Figure 4.5 The TLB EntryLo & EntryHi Registers

Virtual Address Translation

During virtual–to–physical address translation, the R2000 compares the PID and the highest 20 bits (the VPN) of the virtual address to the contents of the TLB. Figure 4.6 illustrates the TLB address translation process.

A virtual address matches a TLB entry when the virtual page number (VPN) field of the virtual address equals the VPN field of the entry, and either the Global (G) bit of the TLB entry is set, or the process identifier (PID) field of the virtual address (as held in the EntryHi register) matches the PID field of the TLB entry. While the Valid (V) bit of the entry must be set for a valid translation to take place, it is not involved in the determination of a matching TLB entry.

If a TLB entry matches, the physical address and access control bits (N, D, and V) are retrieved from the matching TLB entry. Otherwise, a TLB miss (or UTLB miss) exception occurs. If the access control bits (D and V) indicate that the access is not valid, a TLB modification or TLB miss exception occurs. If the N bit is set, the physical address that is retrieved is used to access main memory, bypassing the cache.

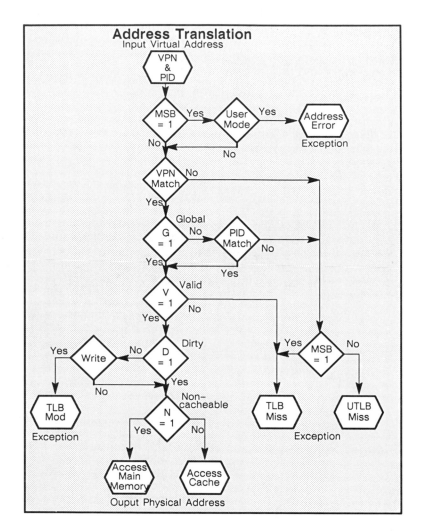

Figure 4.6   TLB Address Translation

The Index Register

The *Index* register is a 32-bit, read/write register, which has 6 bits that index an entry in the TLB. The high-order bit of the register shows the success or failure of a **TLB Probe (tlbp)** instruction (described later in this chapter).

The *Index* register also specifies the TLB entry that will be affected by the **TLB Read (tlbr)** and **TLB Write Index (tlbwi)** instructions. Figure 4.7 shows the format of the *Index* register.

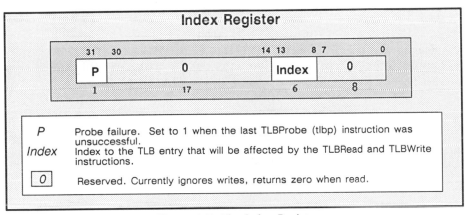

Figure 4.7 The Index Register

The Random Register

The *Random* register is a 32–bit register. The format of the Random register is shown in Figure 4.8. The six-bit *Random* field indexes a random entry in the TLB. The R2000 decrements the *Random* field during every machine cycle but constrains the value of this field to the TLB indexes from 63 to 8 (the counter wraps around from 8 to 63, skipping values 7 through 0).

The **TLB Write Random (tlbwr)** instruction is used to write the TLB entry that this register indexes. The first eight entries (0 to 7) are the "safe" entries because a **tlbwr** instruction can never replace the contents of these entries. Typically, these eight entries are reserved for use by the operating system.

Although normal operations never require it, the contents of this register can be read to verify proper operation of the process. To further simplify testing, the *Random* field is set to a value of 63 when the R2000 is reset.

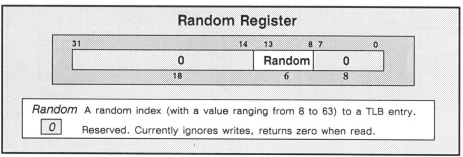

Figure 4.8 The Random Register

TLB Instructions

The instructions that the R2000 provides for working with the TLB are listed in Table 4.1 and described briefly below.

Op Code	Description
tlbp	Translation Lookaside Buffer Probe
tlbr	Translation Lookaside Buffer Read
tlbwi	Translation Lookaside Buffer Write Index
tlbwr	Translation Lookaside Buffer Write Random

Table 4.1 TLB Instructions

Translation Lookaside Buffer Probe (tlbp). This instruction probes the TLB to see if an entry matches the *EntryHi* register contents. If a match exists, the R2000 loads the *Index* register with the index of the entry that matches the *EntryHi* register. When no match exists, the R2000 sets the high order bit (the *P* bit) of the *Index* register.

Translation Lookaside Buffer Read (tlbr). This instruction loads the *EntryHi* and *EntryLo* registers with the contents of the TLB entry specified by the contents of the *Index* register.

Translation Lookaside Buffer Write Index (tlbwi). This instruction loads the specified TLB entry with the contents of the *EntryHi* and *EntryLo* registers. The contents of the Index register specify the TLB entry.

Translation Lookaside Buffer Write Random (tlbwr). This instruction loads a pseudo-randomly specified TLB entry with the contents of the *EntryHi* and *EntryLo* registers. The contents of the *Random* register specify the TLB entry.

5
Exception Processing

This chapter describes how the R2000 Processor handles exceptions and also describes the system control coprocessor (CP0) registers used during exception processing.

When the R2000 detects an exception, the normal sequence of instruction execution is suspended; the processor exits *User mode* and is forced into *Kernel mode* where it can respond to the abnormal or asynchronous event. All events that can initiate exception processing are described in this chapter. Table 5.1 lists the exceptions that the R2000 recognizes.

The R2000's exception handling system efficiently handles machine exceptions, including Translation Lookaside Buffer (TLB) misses, arithmetic overflows, I/O interrupts, and system calls. All of these events interrupt the normal execution flow; the R2000 aborts the instruction causing the exception and also aborts all those following in the instruction pipeline which have already begun execution. The R2000 then performs a direct jump into a designated exception handler routine.

When an exception occurs, the R2000 loads the EPC (Exception Program Counter) with an appropriate restart location where execution may resume after the exception has been serviced. The restart location in the EPC is the address of the instruction which caused the exception or, if the instruction was executing in a branch delay slot, the address of the branch instruction immediately preceding the delay slot.

Exception	Mnemonic	Cause
Reset	Reset	Assertion of the R2000's Reset signal causes an an exception that transfers control to the special vector at virtual address 0xbfc00000.
UTLB miss	UTLB	User TLB miss. A reference is made (in either User mode or Kernel mode) to a page in *kuseg* that has no matching TLB entry.
TLB miss	TLBL (load) TLBS (store)	A referenced TLB entry's Valid bit isn't set or there is a reference to a *kseg2* page that has no matching TLB entry.
TLB modified	Mod	During a store instruction, the Valid bit is set but the Dirty bit is not set.
Bus error	IBE (Instruction) DBE (data)	Assertion of the R2000's BERR* signal due to such external events as bus timeout, backplane bus parity errors, invalid physical addresses or invalid access types.
Address Error	AdEL (load) AdES (store)	Attempt to load, fetch, or store an unaligned word; that is, a word or halfword at an address not evenly divisible by 4 or 2 respectively. Also caused by reference to a virtual address with most significant bit set while in User mode.
Overflow	Ovf	Twos complement overflow during add or subtract.
System call	Sys	Execution of the **syscall** instruction.
Breakpoint	Bp	Execution of the **break** instruction.
Reserved Instruction	RI	Execution of an instruction with an undefined or reserved major operation code (bits 31..26), or a **special** instruction whose minor opcode (bits 5..0) is undefined.
Coprocessor Unusable	CpU	Execution of a coprocessor instruction when the CU (Coprocessor Usable) bit is not set for the target coprocessor.
Interrupt	Int	Assertion of one of the R2000's six hardware interrupt inputs or setting of one of the two software interrupt bits in the Cause register.

Table 5.1 R2000 Exceptions

The Exception Handling Registers

The CP0 registers shown in Figure 5.1 and listed below contain information that is related to exception processing. Software can examine these registers during exception processing to determine such things as the cause of an exception, and the state of the CPU at the time of an exception. Each of these registers is described in detail in the paragraphs that follow.

- the *Cause* register

- the *EPC* (Exception Program Counter) register

- the *Status* register

- the *BadVAddr* (Bad Virtual Address) register

- the *Context* register

- the *PRId* (Processor Revision Identifier) register

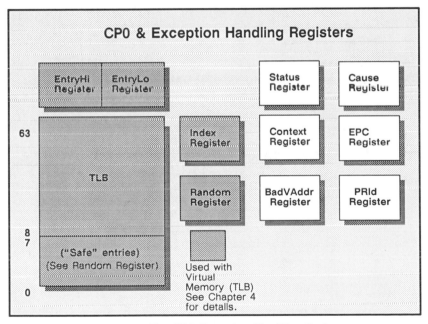

Figure 5.1 The CP0 Exception Handling Registers

Two other registers, the *Index* register and the *Random* register, are used to implement the R2000 virtual memory management system and may also contain information of interest when handling exceptions related to virtual memory errors. Refer to **Chapter 4** for a description of these two registers.

The Cause Register

This contents of this 32–bit register describe the last exception. A 4–bit exception code (ExcCode) indicates the cause as listed in Table 5.2. The remaining fields contain detailed information specific to certain exceptions. All bits in the register, with the exception of the *Sw* bits, are read–only. The Sw bits can be written into to set or reset software interrupts. The format for the *Cause* register is shown in Figure 5.2.

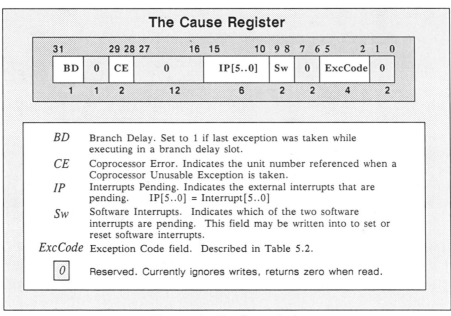

Figure 5.2 The Cause Register

The Cause Register ExcCode Field		
Number	Mnemonic	Description
0	Int	External interrupt
1	MOD	TLB modification exception
2	TLBL	TLB miss exception (Load or instruction fetch)
3	TLBS	TLB miss exception (Store)
4	AdEL	Address error exception (Load or instruction fetch)
5	AdES	Address error exception (Store)
6	IBE	Bus error exception (for an instruction fetch)
7	DBE	Bus error exception (for a data **load** or **store**)
8	Sys	Syscall exception
9	Bp	Breakpoint exception
10	RI	Reserved Instruction exception
11	CpU	Coprocessor Unusable exception
12	Ovf	Arithmetic overflow exception
13–15	—	reserved

Table 5.2 The ExcCode Field

The EPC (Exception Program Counter) Register

The 32-bit, read-only *EPC* register contains the address where processing can resume after an exception has been serviced.

This register contains the virtual address of the instruction that caused the exception. When that instruction resides in a branch delay slot, the *EPC* register contains the virtual address of the immediately preceding **Branch** or **Jump** instruction. The R2000 also sets the *Cause* register's *BD* bit if the exception occurred in the branch delay slot. The *EPC* register format is shown in Figure 5.3.

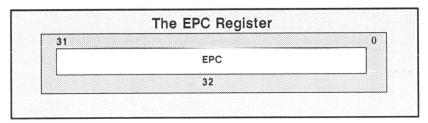

Figure 5.3 The EPC Register

The Status Register

This register contains all major status bits. Any exception puts the system in Kernel mode. All bits in the Status register, with the exception of the *TS* (TLB Shutdown) bit are readable and writeable; the *TS* bit is read-only. Figure 5.4 shows the format of the *Status* register and summarizes the functions performed by each bit. Additional details on the function of each Status register bit are provided in the paragraphs that follow.

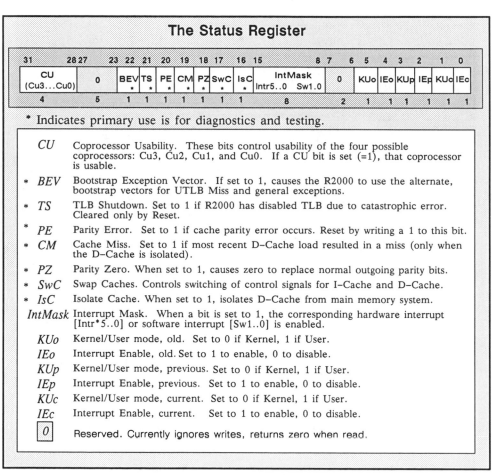

Figure 5.4 *The Status Register*

CU (Coprocessor Usable) controls the usability of each of the possible four coprocessors (Cu3..Cu0). Thus, software can control access of processes to the coprocessors. If a bit is set to 1, the corresponding coprocessor is usable, if a bit is cleared (0), the coprocessor is marked as unusable. All coprocessor instructions require that the target coprocessor be marked usable or a Coprocessor Unusable Exception (described later in this chapter) occurs. Note that the System Control Coprocessor (CP0) is always considered usable when the R2000 is operating in Kernel mode regardless of the setting of the Cu0 bit.

BEV (Bootstrap Exception Vectors) controls location of UTLB miss and general exception vectors during bootstrap (immediately following reset). When this bit is set to 0, the normal exception vectors are used; when the bit is set to 1, bootstrap vector locations are used. This alternate set of vectors can be used when diagnostic tests cause exceptions to occur prior to verifying proper operation of the cache and main memory system. (Refer to **Exception Description Details** later in this chapter for a description of the exception vectors.)

TS (TLB Shutdown). This read–only bit is intended for use by diagnostics and indicates that the R2000 has shut down the TLB due to attempts to access several TLB entries simultaneously. This mechanism protects the TLB from catastrophic hardware failures in the event of software misuse of the TLB — specifically, when two or more TLB entries have the same VPN (Virtual Page Number) and PID (Process ID). When the TLB is in this state, all address translations and TLB probe access are inhibited and have undefined effects. This state can be cleared only by asserting Reset

PE (Parity Error). This bit is set if a cache parity error has occurred. Since the R2000 transparently recovers from parity errors (by taking a cache miss and accessing main memory) this bit is intended for diagnostic purposes. Software can use this bit to log cache parity errors, and diagnostics can use it to verify proper functioning of the cache parity bits and cache parity trees. To clear this bit, write a one to *PE*; writing a zero to this bit does not affect its value.

CM (Cache Miss). This bit is set if the most recent D–Cache load resulted in a cache miss and is intended for use by diagnostic programs to verify the proper functioning of the cache tag and parity bits.. This bit setting only takes effect when in the "isolated cache" mode. See the *IsC* bit.

PZ (Parity Zero). If this bit is set, outgoing parity bits (for both cache data and tags) for store instructions are set to zero

SwC (Swap Caches). This bit controls swapping of the control signals for the data cache (D–Cache) and instruction cache (I–Cache). (0 means normal; 1 means switched.) Cache swapping can be used to implement cache flushing mechanisms and to perform cache testing and diagnostics.

IsC (Isolate Cache). Setting this bit isolates the D–Cache from the main memory system. (0 means normal; 1 means D–Cache isolated.) Cache isolation can be used to implement cache flushing mechanisms and to perform cache testing and diagnostics.

IntMask (Interrupt Mask). These bits allows individual enabling/disabling of each of the eight interrupt classes –– six hardware interrupts and two software interrupts. A 0 in a bit position disables that interrupt and a 1 enables the interrupt. All interrupts can be disabled by clearing the Interrupt Enable bit(s) *IEo/IEp/IEc* described below.

KUo/KUp/KUc (Kernel/User mode: Old/Previous/Current). These three bits comprise a 3–level stack showing the old/previous/current mode (0 means Kernel; 1 means User). Manipulation and use of these bits during exception processing is described in the section that follows.

IEo/IEp/IEc (Interrupt Enable: Old/Previous/Current). These three bits comprise a 3–level stack showing the old/previous/current interrupt enable settings (0 means disable; 1 means enable). Manipulation and use of these bits during exception processing is described in the section that follows.

Status Register Mode Bits and Exception Processing

When the R2000 responds to an exception it saves the *current* Kernel/User mode (KUc) and *current* interrupt enable mode (IEc) bits of the Status register into the *previous* mode bits (KUp and IEp). The *previous* mode bits (KUp and IEp) are saved into the *old* mode bits (KUo and IEo). The *current* mode bits (KUc and IEc) are cleared to cause the processor to enter the Kernel operating mode and turn off interrupts.

This three-level set of mode bits lets the R2000 respond to two levels of exceptions before software must save the contents of the Status register. Figure 5.5 shows how the R2000 manipulates the Status register during exception recognition.

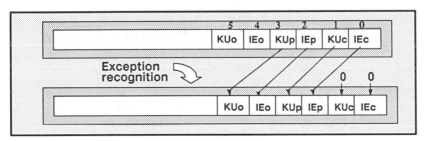

Figure 5.5 The Status Register and Exception Recognition

After an exception handler has completed execution, the R2000 must return to the system context that existed prior to the exception (if possible). The Restore From Exception (**rfe**) instruction provides the mechanism for this return.

The **Restore From Exception** (**rfe**) instruction restores control to a process that an exception pre-empted. When the **rfe** instruction is executed, it restores the "previous" interrupt mask (IEp) bit and Kernel/User mode (KUp) bit in the *Status* register into the the corresponding "current" status bits (IEc and KUc). It also restores the "old" status bits (IEo and KUo) into the corresponding previous status bits (IEp and KUp). The old status bits (IEo and KUo) remain unchanged. The actions of the **rfe** instruction are illustrated in Figure 5.6.

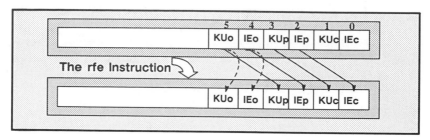

Figure 5.6 Restoring from Exceptions

BadVAddr Register

The *BadVAddr* register saves the entire bad virtual address for any addressing exception: *AdEL* or *AdES*. Figure 5.7 illustrates the organization of the register.

NOTE: This register does not save any information for bus errors since these are not addressing errors.

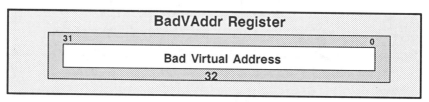

Figure 5.7 The BadVAddr Register

Context Register

The *Context* register duplicates some of the information provided in the *BadVAddr* register, but provides the information in a form that may be more useful for a software TLB exception handler. It is designed for use in a UTLB miss handler, which loads TLB entries for normal user–mode references.

The *Context* register can be used to hold a pointer into the Page Table Entry (PTE). An operating system sets the PTE base field in the register, as needed. Normally, an operating system uses the *Context* register to address the current user process's page map, which resides in the kernel–mapped segment *kseg2*. Note that the use of this register is solely for the convenience of the operating system.

For all addressing exceptions (except bus errors), this register holds the Virtual Page Number (VPN) from the most recent virtual address for which the translation was invalid. Figure 5.8 shows the format of the *Context* register.

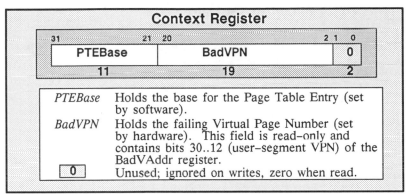

Figure 5.8 The Context Register

Processor Revision Identifier Register

This 32–bit read–only register contains information that identifies the implementation and revision level of the Processor and System Control Coprocessor. The format of the register is shown in Figure 5.9.

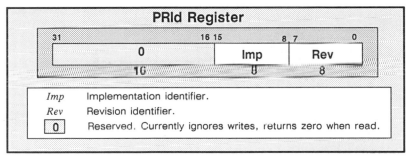

Figure 5.9 The Processor Revision Identifier Register

Exception Description Details

This part of **Chapter 5** describes each exception—its cause, handling, and servicing. **NOTE:** You cannot mask machine exceptions.

Exception Vector Locations

The R2000 uses three different addresses for exception vectors:

- The *RESET* exception vector is at address 0xbfc00000.

- The *UTLB Miss* exception vector is at address 0x8000000.

- The *General* exception vector which is used for all other types of exceptions is at address 0x80000080.

NOTE: If the BEV (Bootstrap Exception Vector) bit in the Status Register is set to 1, the UTLB Miss vector address is changed to 0xbfc00100 and the General exception vector is changed to 0xbfc00180.

Address Error Exception

Cause. This exception occurs when an attempt is made to load, fetch, or store a word that is not aligned on a word boundary. Attempts to load or store a half–word that is not aligned on a half–word boundary also cause this exception. The exception also occurs in User mode if a reference is made to a virtual address whose most significant bit is set—a kernel address. This exception is not maskable.

Handling. The R2000 branches to the General Exception vector (0x80000080) for this exception. When the exception occurs, the R2000 sets the *ADEL* or *ADES* code in the *Cause* register's *ExcCode* field to indicate whether the address error occurred during an instruction fetch or a load operation (*ADEL*) or a store operation (*ADES*).

The *EPC* register points at the instruction that caused the exception, unless the instruction is in a branch delay slot: in that case, the *EPC* register points at the **branch** instruction that preceded the exception–causing instruction and sets the *BD* bit of the *Cause* register.

The R2000 saves the *KUp, IEp, KUc,* and *IEc* bits of the *Status* register in the *KUo, IEo, KUp,* and *IEp* bits, respectively and clears the *KUc* and *IEc* bits.

When this exception occurs, the *BadVAddr* register contains the virtual address that was not properly aligned or that improperly addressed kernel data while in User mode. The contents of the *VPN* field of the *Context* and *EntryHi* registers are undefined.

Surviving. A kernel should hand the executing process a segmentation violation signal. Such an error is usually fatal although an alignment error might be handled by simulating the instruction that caused the error.

Breakpoint Exception

Cause. This exception occurs when the R2000 executes the **BREAK** instruction. This exception is not maskable.

Handling. The R2000 branches to the General Exception vector (0x80000080) for this exception and sets the *BP* code in the *Cause* register's *ExcCode* field.

The R2000 saves the *KUp, IEp, KUc,* and *IEc* bits of the *Status* register in the *KUo, IEo, KUp,* and IEp bits, respectively, and clears the *KUc* and *IEc* bits.

The *EPC* register points at the **BREAK** instruction that caused the exception, unless the instruction is in a branch delay slot: in that case, the *EPC* register points at the **branch** instruction that preceded the **BREAK** instruction and sets the *BD* bit of the *Cause* register.

Servicing. Transfer control to the applicable system routine. Unused bits of the **BREAK** instruction (bits 25..6) can be used to pass additional information. To examine these bits, load the contents of the instruction pointed at by the *EPC* register. **NOTE:** If the instruction resides in the branch delay slot, add four to the contents of the *EPC* register to find the instruction.

To resume execution, change the *EPC* register so that the R2000 does not execute the **BREAK** instruction again. To do this, add four to the *EPC* register before returning. **NOTE:** If a **BREAK** instruction is in the branch delay slot, the **branch** instruction must be interpreted in order to resume execution.

Bus Error Exception

Cause. This exception occurs when the BERR* input to the CPU is asserted by external logic. For example, events like bus time–outs, backplane bus parity errors, and invalid physical memory addresses or access types can signal this exception. This exception is not maskable.

This exception is used for synchronously occurring events such as cache miss refills, uncached references, and unbuffered writes. The general interrupt mechanism must be used to report a bus error that results from asynchronous events such as a buffered write transaction.

Handling. The R2000 branches to the General Exception vector (0x80000080) for this exception. When the exception occurs, the R2000 sets the *IBE* or *DBE* code in the *Cause* register's *ExcCode* field to indicate whether the error occurred during an instruction fetch reference (IBE) or during a data load or store reference (*DBE*).

The *EPC* register points at the instruction that caused the exception, unless the instruction is in a branch delay slot: in that case, the *EPC* register points at the **branch** instruction that preceded the exception–causing instruction and sets the *BD* bit of the *Cause* register.

The R2000 saves the *KUp, IEp, KUc,* and *IEc* bits of the *Status* register in the *KUo, IEo, KUp,* and IEp bits, respectively, and clears the *KUc* and *IEc* bits.

Servicing. The physical address where the fault occurred can be computed from the information in the CPU registers:

- If the *Cause* register's *IBE* code is set (showing an instruction fetch reference), the virtual address resides in the *EPC* register.

- If the *Cause* register's *DBE* exception code is set (specifying a load or store reference), the *instruction* that caused the exception is at the virtual address contained in the *EPC* register (if the *BD* bit of the *Cause* register is set, add four to the contents of the *EPC* register). Interpret the instruction pointed to by *EPC* to get the virtual address of the load or store reference and then use the **TLBProbe (tlbp)** instruction and read *EntryLo* to compute the physical page number.

A kernel should hand the executing process a bus error when this exception occurs. Such an error is usually fatal.

Coprocessor Unusable Exception

Cause. This exception occurs due to an attempt to execute a coprocessor instruction when the corresponding coprocessor unit has not been marked usable (the appropriate *CU* bit in the *Status* register has not been set). For CP0 instructions, this exception occurs when the unit has not been marked usable and the process is executing in User mode: CP0 is always usable from Kernel mode regardless of the setting of the *Cu0* bit in the *Status* register. This exception is not maskable.

Handling. The R2000 branches to the General Exception vector (0x80000080) for this exception. It sets the *CpU* code in the *Cause* register's *ExcCode* field. Only one coprocessor can fail at a time.

The contents of the *Cause* register's *CE* (Coprocessor Error) field show which of the four coprocessors (3, 2, 1, or 0) the R2000 referenced when the exception occurred.

The *EPC* register points at the coprocessor instruction that caused the exception, unless the instruction is in a branch delay slot: in that case, the *EPC* register points at the **branch** instruction that preceded the coprocessor instruction and sets the *BD* bit of the *Cause* register.

The R2000 saves the *KUp, IEp, KUc,* and *IEc* bits of the *Status* register in the *KUo, IEo, KUp,* and *IEp* bits, respectively, and clears the *KUc* and *IEc* bits.

Servicing. To identify the coprocessor unit that was referenced, examine the contents of the *Cause* register's *CE* field. If the process is entitled to access, mark the coprocessor usable and restore the corresponding user state to the coprocessor.

If the process is entitled to access to the coprocessor, but the coprocessor is known not to exist or to have failed, the system could interpret the coprocessor instruction. If the *BD* bit is set in the *Cause* register, the **branch** instruction must be interpreted; then, the coprocessor instruction could be emulated with the *EPC* register advanced past the coprocessor instruction.

If the process is not entitled to access to the coprocessor, the process executing at the time should be handed an illegal instruction/privileged instruction fault signal. Such an error is usually fatal.

Interrupt Exception

Cause. This exception occurs when one of eight interrupt conditions (software generates two, hardware generates six) occurs.

Each of the eight external interrupts can be individually masked by clearing the corresponding bit in the *IntMask* field of the *Status* register. All eight of the interrupts can be masked at once by clearing the *IEc* bit in the *Status* register.

Handling. The R2000 branches to the General Exception vector (0x80000080) for this exception. The R2000 sets the *Int* code in the *Cause* register's *ExcCode* field.

The *IP* field in the *Cause* register show which of six external interrupts are pending, and the *SW* field in the *Cause* register shows which of two software interrupts are pending. More than one interrupt can be pending at a time.

The R2000 saves the *KUp, IEp, KUc,* and *IEc* bits of the *Status* register in the *KUo, IEo, KUp,* and *IEp* bits, respectively, and clears the *KUc* and *IEc* bits.

Servicing. If software generates the interrupt, clear the interrupt condition by setting the corresponding *Cause* register bit (*SW1:0*) to zero.

If external hardware generates the interrupt, clear the interrupt condition by alleviating conditions that assert the interrupt signal (INTR*5:0).

Overflow Exception

Cause. This exception occurs when an **ADD ADDI, SUB,** or **SUBI** instruction results in two's complement overflow. This exception is not maskable.

Handling. The R2000 branches to the General Exception vector (0x80000080) for this exception. The R2000 sets the *OV* code of the *Cause* register.

The *EPC* register points at the instruction that caused the exception, unless the instruction is in a branch delay slot: in that case, the *EPC* register points at the **branch** instruction that preceded the exception–causing instruction and sets the *BD* bit of the *Cause* register.

The R2000 saves the *KUp, IEp, KUc,* and *IEc* bits of the *Status* register in the *KUo, IEo, KUp,* and *IEp* bits, respectively, and clears the *KUc* and *IEc* bits.

Servicing. A kernel should hand the executing process a floating point exception or integer overflow error when this exception occurs. Such an error is usually fatal.

Reserved Instruction Exception

Cause. This exception occurs when the R2000 executes an instruction whose major opcode (bits 31..26) is undefined or a **SPECIAL** instruction whose minor opcode (bits 5..0) is undefined.

This exception provides a way to interpret instructions that might be added to or removed from the MIPS processor architecture.

Handling. The R2000 branches to the General Exception vector (0x80000080) for this exception. It sets the *RI* code of the *Cause* register's *ExcCode* field.

The *EPC* register points at the reserved instruction that caused the exception, unless the instruction is in a branch delay slot: in that case, the *EPC* register points at the **branch** instruction that preceded the reserved instruction and sets the *BD* bit of the *Cause* register.

The R2000 saves the *KUp, IEp, KUc,* and *IEc* bits of the *Status* register in the *KUo, IEo, KUp,* and *IEp* bits, respectively, and clears the *KUc* and *IEc* bits.

Servicing. If instruction interpretation is not implemented, the kernel should hand the executing process an illegal instruction/reserved operand fault signal. Such an error is usually fatal.

An operating system can interpret the undefined instruction and pass control to a routine that implements the instruction in software. If the undefined instruction is in the branch delay slot, the routine that implements the instruction is responsible for simulating the branch instruction after the undefined instruction has been "executed". Simulation of the branch instruction includes determining if the conditions of the branch were met and transferring control to the branch target address (if required) or to the instruction following the delay slot if the branch is not taken. If the branch is not taken, the next instruction's address is = [EPC] + 8. If the branch is taken, the branch target address is calculated as shown below:

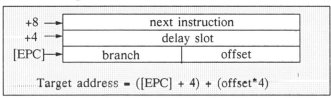

Note that the target address is relative to the address of the instruction in the delay slot, not the address of the branch instruction. Refer to the descriptions of branch instruction for details on how branch target addresses are calculated.

Reset Exception

Cause. This exception occurs when the R2000's RESET signal is asserted and then de-asserted.

Handling. The R2000 provides a special interrupt vector (0xbfc00000) for this exception. The Reset vector resides in the R2000's unmapped and uncached address space; therefore the hardware need not initialize the Translation Lookaside Buffer (TLB) or the cache to handle this exception. The processor can fetch and execute instructions while the caches and virtual memory are in an undefined state.

The contents of all registers in the R2000 are undefined when this exception occurs except for the following:

- The *TS, SWc, KUc*, and *IEc* bits of the *Status* register are cleared to zero.

- The *BEV* bit of the *Status* register is set to one.

- The *Random* register is initialized to 63.

Servicing. The Reset exception is serviced by initializing all processor registers, coprocessor registers, the caches, and the memory system. Typically, diagnostics would then be executed and the operating system bootstrapped. The Reset exception vector is selected to appear within the uncached, unmapped memory space of the machine so that instructions can be fetched and executed while the cache and virtual memory system are still in an undefined state.

System Call Exception

Cause. This exception occurs when the R2000 executes a **SYSCALL** instruction.

Handling. The R2000 branches to the General Exception vector (0x80000080) for this exception and sets the *Sys* code in the *Cause* register's *ExcCode* field.

The *EPC* register points at the **SYSCALL** instruction that caused the exception, unless the **SYSCALL** instruction is in a branch delay slot: in that case, the *EPC* register points at the **branch** instruction that preceded the **SYSCALL** instruction and the *BD* bit of the *Cause* register is set.

The R2000 saves the *KUp, IEp, KUc,* and *IEc* bits of the *Status* register in the *KUo IEo, KUp,* and *IEp bits*, respectively, and clears the *KUc* and *IEc* bits.

Servicing. The operating system transfers control to the applicable system routine. To resume execution, alter the *EPC* register so that the **SYSCALL** instruction does not execute again. To do this, add four to the *EPC* register before returning. **NOTE:** If a **SYSCALL** instruction is in a branch delay slot, the branch instruction must be interpreted in order to resume execution.

TLB Miss Exceptions

There are three different types of TLB misses than can occur:

- If the input Virtual Page Number (VPN) does not match the VPN of any TLB entry, or if the Process Identifier (PID) in *EntryHi* does not match the TLB entry's PID (and the Global bit is not set), a miss occurs. For *kuseg*, a UTLB Miss occurs. For *kseg2*, a TLB Miss occurs.
- If everything matches, but the Valid bit of the matching TLB entry is not set, a TLB Miss occurs.
- If the dirty bit in a matching TLB entry is not set and the access is a write, a TLB MOD exception occurs.

Figure 5.10 (a simplified version of TLB address translation figure used in Chapter 4) illustrates how the three different kinds of TLB miss exceptions are generated. Each of the exceptions is described in detail in the pages that follow.

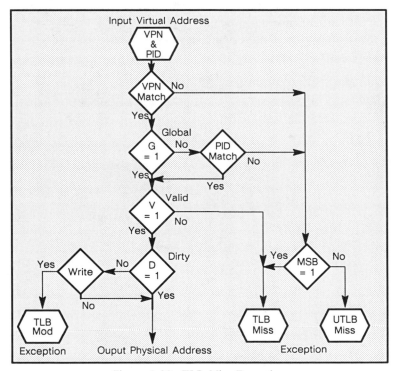

Figure 5.10 TLB Miss Exceptions

TLB Miss Exception

Cause. This exception occurs when a Kernel mode virtual address reference to memory is not mapped, when a User mode virtual address reference to memory matches an invalid TLB entry, or when a Kernel mode reference to user memory space matches an invalid TLB entry.

Handling. The R2000 branches to the General Exception vector (0x80000080) for this exception. When the exception occurs, the R2000 sets the *TLBL* or *TLBS* code in the *Cause* register's *ExcCode* field to indicate whether the miss was due to an instruction fetch or a load operation (*TLBL*) or a store operation (*TLBS*).

The *EPC* register points at the instruction that caused the exception, unless the instruction is in a branch delay slot: in that case, the *EPC* register points at the **branch** instruction that preceded the exception-causing instruction and sets the *BD* bit of the *Cause* register.

The R2000 saves the *KUp, IEp, KUc,* and *IEc* bits of the *Status* register in the *KUo, IEo, KUp,* and *IEp* bits, respectively, and clears the *KUc* and *IEc* bits.

When this exception occurs, the *BadVAddr, Context,* and *EntryHi* registers contain the virtual address that failed address translation. The PID field of *EntryHi* remains unchanged by this exception. The *Random* register normally specifies the pseudo-random location where the R2000 can put a replacement TLB entry.

Servicing. The failing virtual address or virtual page number identifies the corresponding PTE. The operating system should load *EntryLo* with the appropriate PTE that contains the physical page frame and access control bits and also write the contents of *EntryLo* and *EntryHi* into the TLB.

Servicing Multiple (nested) TLB Misses. Within a UTLB Miss handler, the virtual address that specifies the PTE contains physical address and access control information that might not be mapped in the TLB. Then, a TLB Miss exception occurs. You can recognize this case by noting that the *EPC* register points within the UTLB Miss handler. The operating system might interpret the event as an address error (when the virtual address falls outside the valid region for the process) or as a TLB Miss on the page mapping table.

This second TLB miss obscures the contents of the *BadVAddr, Context,* and *EntryHi* registers as they were within the UTLB Miss handler. As a result, the exact virtual address whose translation caused the first fault is not known unless the UTLB Miss handler specifically saved this address. You can only observe the failing PTE virtual address. The *BadVAddr* register now contains the original contents of the *Context* register within the UTLB Miss handler, which is the PTE address for the original faulting address.

If the operating system interprets the exception as a TLB Miss on the page mapping table, it constructs a TLB entry to map the page table and writes the entry into the TLB. Then, the operating system can determine the original faulting virtual page number, but not the complete address. The operating system uses this information to fetch the PTE that contains the physical address and access control information. It also writes this information into the TLB.

The UTLB Miss handler *must* save the EPC in a way that allows the second miss to find it. The *EPC* register information that the UTLB Miss handler saved gives the correct address at which to resume execution. The "old" *KUo* and *IEo* bits of the *Status* register contain the correct mode after the R2000 services a double miss. **NOTE:** You neither need nor want to return to the the UTLB Miss handler at this point.

TLB Modified Exception

Cause. This exception occurs when a store operation's virtual address reference to memory matches a TLB entry that is marked valid, but not marked dirty. This exception is not maskable.

Handling. The R2000 branches to the General Exception vector (0x80000080) for this exception and sets the *MOD* exception code in the *Cause* register's *ExcCode* field.

When this exception occurs, the *BadVAddr*, *Context*, and *EntryHi* registers contain the virtual address that failed address translation. *EntryHi* also contains the PID from which the translation fault occurred.

The *EPC* register points at the instruction that caused the exception, unless the instruction is in a branch delay slot: in that case, the *EPC* register points at the **branch** instruction that preceded the exception–causing instruction and sets the *BD* bit of the *Cause* register.

The R2000 saves the *KUp, IEp, KUc,* and *IEc* bits of the *Status* register in the *KUo, IEo, KUp,* and *IEp* bits, respectively, and clears the *KUc* and *IEc* bits.

Servicing. A kernel should use the failing virtual address or virtual page number to identify the corresponding access control information. The identified page might or might not permit write accesses. (Typically, software maintains the "real" write protection in unused hardware bits.) If the page does not permit write access, a "Write Protection Violation" occurs.

If the page does permit write accesses, the kernel should mark the page frame as dirty in its own data structures. Use the **TLBProbe (tlbp)** instruction to put the index of the TLB entry that must be altered in the *Index* register. Then load the *EntryLo* register with a word that contains the physical page frame and access control bits (with the data bit *D* set). Finally, use the **TLBWrite Indexed (tlbwi)** instruction to write *EntryHi* and *EntryLo* into the TLB.

UTLB Miss Exception

Cause. This exception occurs from Use₁ or Kernel mode references to user memory space when no TLB entry matches both the VPN and the PID. Invalid entries cause a TLB Miss rather than a UTLB Miss. This exception is not maskable.

Handling. The R2000 uses the special ULTB Miss interrupt vector (0x80000000) for this exception. When the exception occurs, the R2000 sets the *TLBL* or *TLBS* code in the *Cause* register's *ExcCode* field to indicate whether the miss was due to an instruction fetch or a load operation (*TLBL*) or a store operation (*TLBS*).

The *EPC* register points at the instruction that caused the exception, unless the instruction is in a branch delay slot: in that case, the *EPC* register points at the **branch** instruction that preceded the exception–causing instruction and sets the *BD* bit of the *Cause* register.

The R2000 saves the *KUp, IEp, KUc,* and *IEc* bits of the *Status* register in the *KUo, IEo, KUp,* and *IEp* bits, respectively, and clears the *KUc* and *IEc* bits.

The virtual address that failed translation is held in the *BadVAddr, Context,* and *EntryHi* registers. The *EntryHi* register also contains the PID (Process Identifier) from which the translation fault occurred. The *Random* register contains a valid psuedo–random location in which to put a replacement TLB entry.

Servicing. The contents of the *Context* register can be used as the virtual address of the memory word that contains the physical page frame and the access control bits—a Page Table Entry (PTE)––for the failing reference. An operating system should put the memory word in *EntryLo* and write the contents of *EntryHi* and *EntryLo* into the TLB by using a **TLB Write Random (tlbwr)** assembly instruction.

The PTE virtual address might be on a page that is not resident in the TLB. Therefore, before an operating system can reference the PTE virtual address, it should save the *EPC* register's contents in a general register reserved for kernel use or in a physical memory location. If the reference is not mapped in the TLB, a TLB Miss exception would occur within the UTLB Miss handler.

R2010 FPA Overview

The R2010 Floating–Point Accelerator (FPA) operates as a coprocessor for the R2000 Processor and extends the R2000's instruction set to perform arithmetic operations on values in floating–point representations. The R2010 FPA, with associated system software, fully conforms to the requirements of ANSI/IEEE Standard 754–1985, "IEEE Standard for Binary Floating–Point Arithmetic." In addition, the MIPS architecture fully supports the standard's recommendations. Figure 6.1 illustrates the functional organization of the FPA.

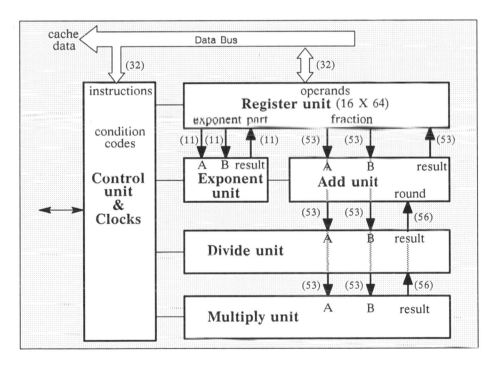

Figure 6.1   R2010 FPA Functional Block Diagram

R2010 FPA Features

- **Full 64–bit Operation**. The R2010 contains sixteen, 64–bit registers that can each be used to hold single–precision or double–precision values. The FPA also includes a 32–bit status/control register that provides access to all IEEE–Standard exception handling capabilities.

- **Load/Store Instruction Set**. Like the R2000 Processor, the R2010 uses a load/store–oriented instruction set, with single–cycle loads and stores. Floating–point operations are started in a single cycle and their execution is overlapped with other fixed point or floating–point operations.

- **Tightly–coupled Coprocessor Interface** – the FPA connects to the R2000 Processor to form a tightly–coupled unit with a seamless integration of floating–point and fixed–point instruction sets. Since each unit receives and executes instructions in parallel, some floating–point instructions can execute at the same single–cycle per instruction rate as fixed point–instructions.

R2010 FPA Programming Model

This section describes the organization of data in registers and in memory and the set of general registers available. This section also gives a summary description of all the R2010 FPA registers.

The R2010 FPA provides three types of registers as shown in Figure 6.2:

- Floating–Point General–Purpose Registers (FGR)
- Floating–Point Registers (FPR)
- Floating–Point Control Registers (FCR)

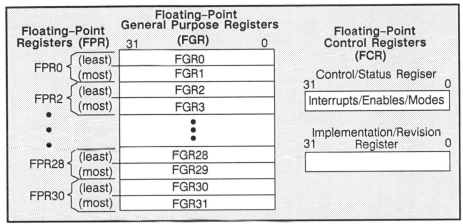

Figure 6.2 R2010 FPA Registers

Floating–Point General–Purpose Registers (FGR) are directly addressable, physical registers. The FPA provides thirty–two 32–bit FGRs.

Floating–Point Registers (FPR) are logical registers used to store data values during floating–point operations. Each of the 16 FPRs is 64 bits wide and is formed by concatenating two adjacent FGRs. Depending on the requirements of an operation, FPRs hold either single– or double–precision floating–point values.

Floating–Point Control Registers are used for rounding mode control, exception handling, and state saving. The FCRs include the Control/Status register and the Implementation/Revision register.

Floating–Point General Registers

The 32 Floating–Point General Registers (FGRs) on the FPA are directly addressable 32–bit registers used in floating–point operations and individually accessible via move, load, and store instructions. The FGRs are listed in Table 6.1, and the Floating Point Registers (FPRs) that are logically formed by the general registers are described in the section that follow.

Table 6.1 Floating–Point General Registers

FGR Number	Usage
0	FPR 0 (least)
1	FPR 0 (most)
2	FPR 2 (least)
3	FPR 2 (most)
•	•
•	•
•	•
28	FPR 28 (least)
29	FPR 28 (most)
30	FPR 30 (least)
31	FPR 30 (most)

Floating–Point Registers

The R2010 provides 16 Floating–Point Registers (FPR). These logical 64–bit registers hold floating–point values during floating–point operations and are physically formed from the General–Purpose Registers (FGR).

The FPRs hold values in either single– or double–precision floating–point format. Only even numbers are used to address FPRs: odd FPR register numbers are invalid. During single–precision floating–point operations, only the even–numbered (least) general registers are used, and during double–precision floating–point operations, the general registers are accessed in double pairs. Thus, in a double–precision operation, selecting Floating–Point Register 0 (FPR0) addresses adjacent Floating–Point General–Purpose Registers FGR0 and FGR1.

Floating–Point Control Registers

MIPS coprocessors can have as many as 32 control registers. The FPA coprocessor implements two Floating–Point Control Registers (FCRs). These registers can be accessed only by Move operations and contain the following:

- The *Control/Status register (FCR31)*, is used to control and monitor exceptions, hold result of compare operations, and establish rounding modes; and

- The *Implementation/Revision register (FCR0)*, holds revision information about the FPA.

Control/Status Register   (Read and Write)

The Control/Status register, FCR31, contains control and status data and can be accessed by instructions running in either Kernel or User mode. It controls the arithmetic rounding mode and the enabling of exceptions. It also indicates exceptions that occurred in the most recently executed instruction, and all exceptions that have occurred since the register was cleared. Figure 6.3 shows the bit assignments.

The Control/Status Register

31	24	23 22	18	17 12	11 7	6 2	1 0
0		C	0	Exceptions E V Z O U I	TrapEnable V Z O U I	Sticky Bits V Z O U I	RM
8		1	5	6	5	5	2

C	Condition bit. Set/cleared to reflect result of Compare instruction and drives the FPA's CpCond output signal.
Exceptions	These bits are set to indicate any exceptions that occurred during the most recent instruction.
TrapEnable	Trap Enables. These bits enable assertion of the CpInt* signal if the corresponding Exception bit is set during a floating-point operation.
Sticky bits	These bits are set if an exception occurs and are reset only by explicitly loading new settings into this register (with a Move instruction)
RM	Rounding Mode. These two bits specify which of the four rounding modes is to be used by the FPA.
0	Reserved. Currently ignores writes, undefined when read.

Figure 6.3   Control/Status Register Bit Assignments

When the Control/Status register is read using a *Move Control From Coprocessor 1* (CFC1) instruction, all unfinished instructions in the pipeline are completed before the contents of the register are moved to the main processor. If a floating-point exception occurs as the pipeline empties, the exception is taken and the CFC1 instruction can be re-executed after the exception is serviced.

The bits in the Control/Status register can be set or cleared by writing to the register using a *Move Control To Coprocessor 1* (CTC1) instruction. This register must only be written to when the FPA is not actively executing floating-point operations: this can be assured by first reading the contents of the register to empty the pipeline.

Control/Status Register Condition Bit

Bit 23 of the Control/Status register is the *Condition* bit. When a floating–point *Compare* operation takes place, the detected condition is placed at bit 23, so that the state of the condition line may be saved or restored. The "C" bit is set (1) if the condition is true and cleared (0) if the condition is false. Bit 23 is affected only by *Compare* and *Move Control To FPA* instructions.

Control/Status Register Exception Bits

Bits 17:12 in the Control/Status register contains *Exception* bits as shown in Figure 6.4 that reflect the results of the most recently executed instruction. These bits are appropriately set or cleared after each floating–point operation. Exception bits are set for instructions that cause one of the five IEEE standard exceptions or the Unimplemented Operation exception.

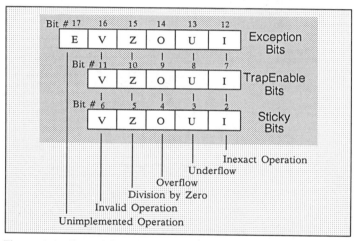

Figure 6.4 Control/Status Register Exception/Sticky/TrapEnable Bits

If two exceptions occur together in one instruction, both of the appropriate bits in the exception bit field will be set. When an exception occurs, both the corresponding *Exception* and *Sticky* bits are set. Refer to **Chapter 8, Floating Point Exceptions**, for a complete description of floating–point exceptions.

The Unimplemented Operation exception is not one of the standard IEEE–defined floating–point exceptions. It is provided to permit software implementation of IEEE standard operations and exceptions that are not fully supported by the FPA. Note that trapping on this exception cannot be disabled: there is no *TrapEnable* bit for *E*.

Control/Status Register Sticky Bits

The *Sticky* bits shown in Figure 6.4 hold the accumulated or accrued exception bits required by the IEEE standard for *trap disabled* operation. These bits are set whenever an FPA operation result causes one of the corresponding *Exception* bits to be set. However, unlike the *Exception* bits, the *Sticky* bits are never cleared as a side-effect of floating–point operations; they can be cleared only by writing a new value into the Control/Status register, using the *Move Control To Coprocessor 1* (CTC1) instruction.

Control/Status Register TrapEnable Bits

The *TrapEnable* bits shown in Figure 6.4 are used to enable a user trap when an exception occurs during a floating–point operation. If the TrapEnable bit corresponding to the exception is set it causes assertion of the FPA's CpInt* signal. The R2000 responds to the CpInt* signal by taking an interrupt exception which can then be used to implement trap handling of the FPA exception.

Control/Status Register Rounding Mode Control Bits

Bits 1 and 0 in the Control/Status register comprise the Rounding Mode (*RM*) field. These bits specify the rounding mode that the FPA will use for all floating–point operations as shown in Table 6.2.

RM Bits	Mnemonic	Rounding Mode Description
00	RN	Rounds result to nearest representable value; round to value with least significant bit zero when the two nearest representable values are equally near.
01	RZ	Rounds result toward zero; round to value closest to and not greater in magnitude than the infinitely precise result.
10	RP	Rounds toward $+\infty$; round to value closest to and not less than the infinitely precise result.
11	RM	Rounds toward $-\infty$; round to value closest to and not greater than the infinitely precise result.

Table 6.2 Rounding Mode Bit Decoding

Implementation and Revision Register (Read Only)

The FPA control register zero (FCR0) contains values that define the implementation and revision number of the R2010 FPA. This information can be used to determine the coprocessor revision and performance level and can also used by diagnostic software. NOTE: This register is intended to assist users in identifying version-specific characteristics of the FPA. However, due to the variety of levels at which design changes may be implemented to the silicon, the revision information cannot be guaranteed with every revision of the device nor assured to follow a completely predictable numerical sequence. MIPS has complete discretion over defining these characteristics of the FPA.

Only the low-order bytes of the implementation and revision register are defined. Bits 15 through 8 identify the implementation and bits 7 through 0 identify the revision number as shown in Figure 6.5.

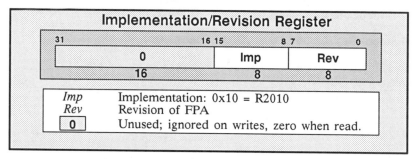

Figure 6.5 Implementation/Revision Register

Floating-Point Formats

The R2010 FPA performs both 32-bit (single-precision) and 64-bit (double-precision) IEEE standard floating-point operations. The 32-bit format has a 24-bit signed-magnitude fraction field and an 8-bit exponent, as shown in Figure 6.6.

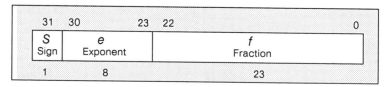

Figure 6.6 Single-Precision Floating-Point Format

The 64–bit format has a 53–bit signed–magnitude fraction field and an 11–bit exponent, as shown in Figure 6.7.

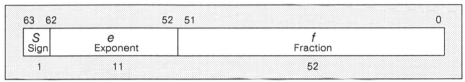

Figure 6.7 Double–Precision Floating–Point Format

Numbers in the single–precision and double–precision floating–point formats (extended and quad formats are not supported by R2010 FPA) are composed of three fields:

- A 1–bit sign: s,
- A biased exponent: $e = E + bias$, and
- A fraction: $f = .b_1 b_2 ... b_{p-1}$

The range of the unbiased exponent E includes every integer between two values E_{min} and E_{max} inclusive, and also two other reserved values: $E_{min} - 1$ to encode ± 0 and denormalized numbers, and $E_{max} + 1$ to encode $\pm \infty$ and NaNs (Not a Number). For single– and double–precision formats, each representable non–zero numerical value has just one encoding.

For single– and double–precision formats, the value of a number, v, is determined by the equations shown in Table 6.3.

Table 6.3 Equations for Calculating Values in Floating–Point Format

(1)	if $E = E_{max} + 1$ and $f \neq 0$, then v is NAN, regardless of s.
(2)	if $E = E_{max} + 1$ and $f = 0$, then $v = (-1)^S \infty$.
(3)	if $E_{min} \leq E \leq E_{max}$, then $v = (-1)^S 2^E (1.f)$.
(4)	if $E = E_{min} - 1$ and $f \neq 0$, then $v = (-1)^S 2^{E_{min}} (0.f)$.
(5)	if $E = E_{min} - 1$ and $f = 0$, then $v = (-1)^S 0$.

For all floating–point formats, if v is NaN, the most significant bit of f determines whether the value is a signaling or quiet NaN. v is a signaling NaN if the most significant bit of f is set; otherwise v is a quiet NaN.

Table 6.4 defines the values for the format parameters in the preceding description.

Table 6.4   Floating–Point Format Parameter Values

Parameter	Single	Double
P	24	53
E_{max}	+127	+1023
E_{min}	–126	–1022
exponent *bias*	+127	+1023
exponent width in bits	8	11
integer bit	hidden	hidden
fraction width in bits	23	52
format width in bits	32	64

Number Definitions

This subsection contains a definition of the following number types specified in the IEEE 754 standard:

- Normalized Numbers
- Denormalized Numbers
- Infinity
- Zero

For more information, refer to the *ANSI/IEEE Std 754–1985 IEEE Standard for Binary Floating–Point Arithmetic.*

Normalized Numbers

Most floating–point calculations are performed on normalized numbers. For single–precision operations, normalized numbers have a biased exponent that ranges from 1 to 254 (–126 to +127 unbiased) and a normalized fraction field, meaning that the leftmost, or hidden, bit is one. In decimal notation, this allows representation of a range of positive and negative numbers from approximately 10^{38} to 10^{-38}, with accuracy to 7 decimal places.

Denormalized Numbers

Denormalized numbers have a zero exponent and a denormalized (hidden bit equal to zero) non-zero fraction field.

Infinity

Infinity has an exponent of all ones and a fraction field equal to zero. Both positive and negative infinity are supported.

Zero

Zero has an exponent of zero, a hidden bit equal to zero, and a value of zero in the fraction field. Both +0 and −0 are supported.

Coprocessor Operation

The FPA continually monitors the R2000 Processor instruction stream. If an instruction does not apply to the coprocessor, it is ignored; if an instruction does apply to the coprocessor, the FPA executes that instruction and transfers necessary result and exception data synchronously to the R2000 main processor.

The FPA performs three types of operations:

- Loads and Stores;
- Moves;
- Two- and three-register floating-point operations.

Load, Store, and Move Operations

Load, Store, and Move operations move data between memory or the R2000 Processor registers and the R2010 FPA registers. These operations perform no format conversions and cause no floating-point exceptions. Load, Store, and Move operations reference a single 32-bit word of either the Floating-Point General Registers (FGR) or the Floating-Point Control Registers (FCR).

Floating-Point Operations

The FPA supports the following single- and double-precision format floating-point operations:

- Add
- Subtract
- Multiply
- Divide
- Absolute Value
- Move
- Negate
- Compare

In addition, the FPA supports conversions between single- and double-precision floating-point formats and fixed-point formats. Refer to **Chapter 7** for a complete description of all the FPA instructions.

Exceptions

The R2010 FPA supports all five IEEE standard exceptions:

- Invalid Operation
- Inexact Operation
- Division by Zero
- Overflow
- Underflow

The FPA also supports the optional, Unimplemented Operation exception that allows unimplemented instructions to trap to software emulation routines. For more information on exceptions, refer to **Chapter 8. Floating Point Exceptions**.

Instruction Set Overview

All R2010 instructions are 32 bits long and they can be divided into the following groups:

- **Load/Store and Move** instructions move data between memory, the main processor and the FPA general registers.

- **Computational** instructions perform arithmetic operations on floating point values in the FPA registers.

- **Conversion** instructions perform conversion operations between the various data formats.

- **Compare** instructions perform comparisons of the contents of registers and set a condition bit based on the results.

Table 6.5 lists the instruction set of the R2010 FPA. A more detailed summary is contained in **Chapter 7** and a complete description of each instruction is provided in **Appendix B**.

OP	Description	OP	Description
	Load/Store/Move Instructions		**Computational Instructions**
LWC1	Load Word to FPA	ADD.fmt	Floating–point Add
SWC1	Store Word from FPA	SUB.fmt	Floating–point Subtract
MTC1	Move word To FPA	MUL.fmt	Floating–point Multiply
MFC1	Move word From FPA	DIV.fmt	Floating–point Divide
CTC1	Move Control word To FPA	ABS.fmt	Floating–point Absolute value
CFC1	Move Control word From FPA	MOV.fmt	Floating–point Move
		NEG.fmt	Floating–point Negate
	Conversion Instructions		**Compare Instructions**
CVT.S.fmt	Floating–point Convert to Single FP	C.cond.fmt	Floating–point Compare
CVT.D.fmt	Floating–point Convert to Double FP		
CVT.W.fmt	Floating–point Convert to fixed–point		

Table 6.5 R2010 Instruction Summary

R2010 Pipeline Architecture

The R2010 FPA provides an instruction pipeline that parallels that of the R2000 Processor. The FPA, however, has a 6–stage pipeline instead of the 5–stage pipeline of the R2000: the additional FPA pipe stage is used to provide efficient coordination of exception responses between the FPA and main processor.

The execution of a single R2010 instruction consists of six primary steps:

1) **IF**—Instruction Fetch. The main processor calculates the instruction address required to read an instruction from the I–Cache. No action is required of the FPA during this pipe stage since the main processor is responsible for address generation.

2) **RD**—The instruction is present on the data bus during phase 1 of this pipe stage, and the FPA decodes the data on the bus to determine if it is an instruction for the FPA.

3) **ALU**—If the instruction is an FPA instruction, instruction execution commences during this pipe stage.

4) **MEM**—If this is a coprocessor load or store instruction, the FPA presents or captures the data during phase 2 of this pipe stage.

5) **WB**—The FPA uses this pipe stage solely to deal with exceptions.

6) **FWB**—The FPA uses this stage to write back ALU results to its register file. This stage is the equivalent of the WB stage in the R2000 main processor.

Each of these steps requires approximately one FPA cycle as shown in Figure 6.8 (parts of some operations spill over into another cycle while other operations require only 1/2 cycle).

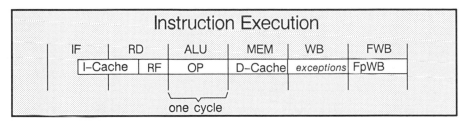

Figure 6.8 Instruction Execution Sequence

The R2010 uses a 6–stage pipeline to achieve an instruction execution rate approaching one instruction per FPA cycle. Thus, execution of six instructions at a time are overlapped as shown in Figure 6.9.

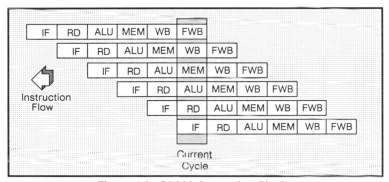

Figure 6.9 R2010 Instruction Pipeline

This pipeline operates efficiently because different FPA resources (address and data bus accesses, ALU operations, register accesses, and so on) are utilized on a non–interfering basis. Refer to **Chapter 7** for a detailed discussion of the instruction pipeline.

FPA Instruction Set Summary
& Instruction Pipeline

This chapter provides an summary of the R2010 FPA's instruction set and also includes a detailed discussion of the FPA's instruction pipeline that permits overlapping of instructions to increase the effective instruction execution rate.

Instruction Set Summary

The floating point instructions supported by the R2010 FPA are all implemented using the coprocessor unit 1 (COP1) operation instructions of the R2000 Processor instruction set. The basic operations performed by the FPA are:

- Load and store operations from/to the FPA registers
- Moves between FPA and CPU registers
- Computational operations including floating–point add, subtract, multiply, divide, and convert instructions
- Floating point comparisons

NOTE: The *branch on coprocessor 1 condition* (**BC1T/BC1F**) operations are also COP1 operations and are described in this chapter: however, these instructions are actually implemented entirely by the R2000 Processor using the CpCond input from the FPA.

Load, Store, and Move Instructions

All movement of data between the R2010 FPA and memory is accomplished by load word to coprocessor 1 (**LWC1**) and store word to coprocessor 1 (**SWC1**) instructions which reference a single 32–bit word of the FPA's general registers. These loads and stores are unformatted; no format conversions are performed and therefore no floating–point exceptions occur due to these operations.

Data may also be directly moved between the FPA and the R2000 Processor by *move to coprocessor 1* (**MTC1**) and *move from coprocessor 1* (**MFC1**) instructions. Like the floating–point load and store operations, these operations perform no format conversions and never cause floating–point exceptions.

The *load* and *move to* operations have a latency of one instruction. That is, the data being loaded from memory or the CPU into an FPA register is not available to the instruction that immediately follows the load instruction: the data is available to the second instruction after the load instruction. (Refer to **R2010 Instruction Pipeline** at the end of this chapter for a detailed discussion of load instruction latency.)

Table 7.1 summarizes the R2010 Load, Store and Move instructions.

Instruction	Format and Description
Load Word to FPA (coprocessor 1)	*LWC1 ft,offset(base)* Sign–extend 16–bit *offset* and add to contents of CPU register *base* to form address. Load contents of addressed word into FPA general register *ft.*
Store Word from FPA (coprocessor 1)	*SWC1 ft,offset(base)* Sign–extend 16–bit *offset* and add to contents of CPU register *base* to form address. Store 32–bit contents of FPA general register *ft* at addressed location.
Move Word to FPA (coprocessor 1)	*MTC1 rt,fs* Move contents of CPU register *rt* into FPA register *fs.*
Move Word from FPA (coprocessor 1)	*MFC1 rt,fs* Move contents of FPA general register *fs* into CPU register *rt.*
Move Control Word to FPA (coprocessor 1)	*CTC1 rt,fs* Move contents of CPU register *rt* into FPA control register *fs.*
Move Control Word from FPA (coprocessor 1)	*CFC1 rt,fs* Move contents of FPA control register *fs* into CPU register *rt.*

Table 7.1   R2010 FPA Load, Store and Move Instruction Summary

Floating Point Computational Instructions

Computational instructions perform arithmetic operations on floating–point values in registers. There are four categories of computational instructions summarized in Table 7.2:

- **3–Operand Register–Type** instructions that perform floating point addition, subtraction, multiplication, and division operations

- **2–Operand Register–Type** instructions that perform floating point absolute value, move, and negate operations

- **Convert** instructions that perform conversions between the various data formats

- **Compare** instructions that perform comparisons of the contents of two registers and set or clear a condition signal based on the result of the comparison.

In the instruction formats shown in Table 7.2, the *fmt* term appended to the instruction op code is the data format specifier: *s* specifies Single–precision binary floating–point, *d* specifies Double–precision binary floating–point, and *w* specifies binary fixed–point. For example, an **ADD.d** specifies that the operands for the addition operation are double–precision binary floating–point values. NOTE: when fmt is single–precision or binary fixed point, the odd register of the destination is undefined.

Instruction	Format and Description
Floating-point Add	*ADD.fmt* *fd,fs,ft* Interpret contents of FPA registers *fs* and *ft* in specified format *(fmt)* and add arithmetically. Place rounded result in FPA register *fd.*
Floating-point Subtract	*SUB.fmt* *fd,fs,ft* Interpret contents of FPA registers *fs* and *ft* in specified format *(fmt)* and arithmetically subtract *ft* from *fs.* Place result in FPA register *fd.*
Floating-point Multiply	*MUL.fmt* *fd,fs,ft* Interpret contents of FPA registers *fs* and *ft* in specified format *(fmt)* and arithmetically multiply *ft* and *fs.* Place result in FPA register *fd.*
Floating-point Divide	*DIV.fmt* *fd,fs,ft* Interpret contents of FPA registers *fs* and *ft* in specified format *(fmt)* and arithmetically divide *fs* by *ft.* Place rounded result in register *fd.*
Floating-point Absolute Value	*ABS.fmt* *fd,fs* Interpret contents of FPA register *fs* in specified format *(fmt)* and take arithmetic absolute value. Place result in FPA register *fd.*
Floating-point Move	*MOV.fmt* *fd,fs* Interpret contents of FPA register *fs* in specified format *(fmt)* and copy into FPA register *fd.*
Floating-point Negate	*NEG.fmt* *fd,fs* Interpret contents of FPA register *fs* in specified format *(fmt)* and take arithmetic negation. Place result in FPA register *fd.*
Floating-point Convert to Single FP Format	*CVT.S.fmt* *fd,fs* Interpret contents of FPA register *fs* in specified format *(fmt)* and arithmetically convert to the single binary floating point format. Place rounded result in FPA register *fd.*
Floating-point Convert to Double FP Format	*CVT.D.fmt* *fd,fs* Interpret contents of FPA register *fs* in specified format *(fmt)* and arithmetically convert to the double binary floating point format. Place rounded result in FPA register *fd.*
Floating-point Convert to Single Fixed-Point Format	*CVT.W.fmt* *fd,fs* Interpret contents of FPA register *fs* in specified format *(fmt)* and arithmetically convert to the single fixed-point format. Place result in FPA register *fd.*
Floating-point Compare	*C.cond.fmt* *fs,ft* Interpret contents of FPA registers *fs* and *ft* in specified format *(fmt)* and arithmetically compare. The result is determined by the comparison and the specified condition *(cond).* After a one instruction delay, the condition is available for testing by the R2000 with the *branch on floating-point coprocessor condition (BC1T,BC1F)* instructions.

Table 7.2 R2010 FPA Computational Instruction Summary

Floating Point Relational Operations

The Floating-point Compare (*C.fmt.cond*) instructions interpret the contents of two FPA registers (*fs, ft*) in the specified format (*fmt*) and arithmetically compares them. A result is determined based on the comparison and conditions (*cond*) specified in the instruction. Table 7.3 lists the conditions that can be specified for the Compare instruction and Table 7.4 summarizes the floating-point relational operations that are performed.

Mnemonic	Definition	Mnemonic	Definition
F	False	T	True
UN	Unordered	OR	Ordered
EQ	Equal	NEQ	Not Equal
UEQ	Unordered or Equal	OLG	Ordered or Less than or Greater than
OLT	Ordered Less Than	UGE	Unordered or Greater than or Equal
ULT	Unordered or Less Than	OGE	Ordered Greater Than
OLE	Ordered Less than or Equal	UGT	Unordered or Greater Than
ULE	Unordered or Less than or Equal	OGT	Ordered Greater Than
SF	Signaling False	ST	Signaling True
NGLE	Not Greater than or Less than or Equal	GLE	Greater than, or Less than or Equal
SEQ	Signaling Equal	SNE	Signaling Not Equal
NGL	Not Greater than or Less than	GL	Greater Than or Less Than
LT	Less Than	NLT	Not Less Than
NGE	Not Greater than or Equal	GE	Greater Than or Equal
LE	Less than or Equal	NLE	Not Less Than or Equal
NGT	Not Greater Than	GT	Greater Than

Table 7.3   Relational Mnemonic Definitions

Table 7.4 is derived from the similar table in the IEEE floating point standard and describes the 26 predicates named in the standard. The table includes six additional predicates (for a total of 32) to round out the set of possible predicates based on the conditions tested by a comparison. Four mutually exclusive relations are possible: less than, equal, greater than, and unordered. Note that invalid operation exceptions occur only when comparisons include the *less than* (<) or *greater than* (>) characters but not the *unordered* (?) character in the ad hoc form of the predicate.

PREDICATES			RELATIONS				Invalid Operation Exception if Unordered
Condition Mnemonic	ad hoc	FORTRAN	Greater Than	Less Than	Equal	Un-ordered	
F	false		F	F	F	F	no
UN	?		F	F	F	T	no
EQ	=	.EQ.	F	F	T	F	no
UEQ	?=	.UE.	F	F	T	T	no
OLT	NOT(?>=)	.NOT. .UG.	F	T	F	F	no
ULT	?<	.UL.	F	T	F	T	no
OLE	NOT(?>)	.NOT. .UG.	F	T	T	F	no
ULE	?<=	.ULE.	F	T	T	T	no
OGT	NOT(?<=)	.NOT. .ULE.	T	F	F	F	no
UGT	?>	.UGT.	T	F	F	T	no
OGE	NOT(?<)	.NOT. .UL.	T	F	T	F	no
UGE	?>=	.UGE.	T	F	T	T	no
OLG	NOT(?=)		T	T	F	F	no
NEQ	NOT(=)	.NE.	T	T	F	T	no
OR	NOT(?)		T	T	T	F	no
T	true		T	T	T	T	no
SF			F	F	F	F	yes
NGLE	NOT(<=>)	.NOT. .LEG.	F	F	F	T	yes
SEQ			F	F	T	F	yes
NGL	NOT(<>)	.NOT. .LG.	F	F	T	T	yes
LT	<	.LT.	F	T	F	F	yes
NGE	NOT(>=)	.NOT. .GE.	F	T	F	T	yes
LE	<=	.LE.	F	T	T	F	yes
NGT	NOT(>)	.NOT. .GT.	F	T	T	T	yes
GT	>	.GT.	T	F	F	F	yes
NLE	NOT(<=)	.NOT. .LE.	T	F	F	T	yes
GE	>=	.GE.	T	F	T	F	yes
NLT	NOT(<)	.NOT. .LT.	T	F	T	T	yes
GL	<>	.LG.	T	T	F	F	yes
SNE			T	T	F	T	yes
GLE	<=>	.LEG.	T	T	T	F	yes
ST			T	T	T	T	yes

Table 7.4   Floating Point Relational Operators

Branch on FPA Condition Instructions

Table 7.5 summarizes the two branch on FPA (coprocessor unit 1) condition instructions that can be used to test the result of the FPA Compare (**C.cond**) instructions.
In this table, the phrase *delay slot* refers to the instruction immediately following the
branch instruction. Refer to the *R2000 Processor User's Guide* for a discussion of the
branch delay slot.

Instruction	Format and Description
Branch on FPA True	*BC1T* Compute a branch target address by adding address of instruction in the delay slot and the 16-bit *offset* (shifted left two bits and sign-extended to 32 bits). Branch to the target address (with a delay of one instruction) if the FPA's CpCond signal is true.
Branch on FPA False	*BC1F* Compute a branch target address by adding address of instruction in the delay slot and the 16-bit *offset* (shifted left two bits and sign-extended to 32 bits). Branch to the target address (with a delay of one instruction) if the FPA's CpCond signal is false.

Table 7.5 Branch on FPA Condition Instructions

The Instruction Pipeline

The R2010 FPA provides an instruction pipeline that parallels that of the R2000 Processor. The FPA, however, has a 6-stage pipeline instead of the 5-stage pipeline of the R2000: the additional FPA pipe stage is used to provide efficient coordination of exception responses between the FPA and main processor. Figure 7.1 illustrates the six stages of the FPA instruction pipeline.

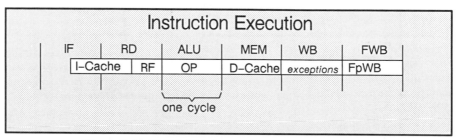

Figure 7.1 R2010 FPA Instruction Execution Sequence

The six stages of the FPA instruction pipeline are used as follows:

1) **IF**—Instruction Fetch. The CPU calculates the instruction address required to read an instruction from the I-Cache. The instruction address is generated and output during phase 2 of this pipe stage. No action is required of the FPA during this pipe stage since the main processor is responsible for address generation. Note that the instruction is not actually read into the processor until the beginning (phase 1) of the RD pipe stage.

2) **RD**—The instruction is present on data bus during phase 1 of this pipe stage and the FPA decodes the data on the bus to determine if it is an instruction for the FPA. The FPA reads any required operands from its registers (RF = Register Fetch) while decoding the instruction.

3) **ALU**—If the instruction is one for the FPA, execution commences during this pipe stage. If the instruction causes an exception, the FPA notifies the R2000 main processor of the exception during this pipe stage by asserting the FpInt* signal. If the FPA determines that it requires additional time to complete this instruction, it initiates a stall during this pipe stage.

4) **MEM**—If this is a coprocessor load or store instruction, the FPA presents or captures the data during phase 2 of this pipe stage. If an interrupt is taken by the main processor, it notifies the FPA during phase 2 of this pipe stage (via the Exception* signal).

5) **WB**—If the instruction that is currently in the write back (WB) stage caused an exception, the main processor notifies the FPA by asserting the Exception* signal during this pipe stage. Thus, the FPA uses this pipe stage solely to deal with exceptions.

6) **FWB**—The FPA uses this stage to write back ALU results to its register file. This stage is the equivalent of the WB stage in the R2000 main processor.

Figure 7.2 illustrates how the six instructions would be overlapped in the FPA pipeline.

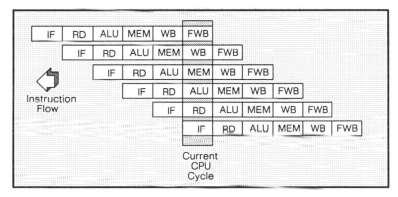

Figure 7.2 R2010 FPA Instruction Pipeline

This figure presumes that each instruction can be completed in a single cycle. Most FPA instructions, however, require more than one cycle to execute. Therefore, the FPA must stall the pipeline if an instruction's execution cannot proceed because of register or resource conflicts. Figure 7.3 illustrates the effect of a three–cycle stall on the FPA pipeline.

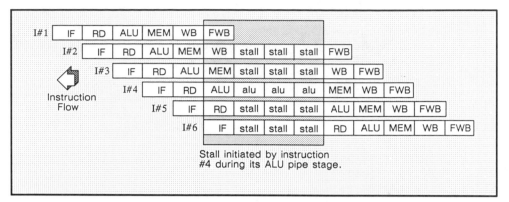

Figure 7.3 An FPA Pipeline Stall

To mitigate the performance impact that would result from frequently stalling the instruction pipeline, the FPA allows overlapping of instructions so that instruction execution can proceed so long as there are no resource conflicts, data dependencies, or exception conditions. The sections that follow describe and illustrate the timing and overlapping of FPA instructions.

Instruction Execution Times

Unlike the R2000 Processor which executes almost all instructions in a single cycle, the time required to execute FPA instructions ranges from one cycle to 19 cycles. Figure 7.4 illustrates the number of cycles required to execute each of the FPA instructions.

In Figure 7.4, the cycles of an instruction's execution time that are darkly shaded █ require exclusive access to an FPA resource (such as buses or ALU) that precludes the concurrent use by another instruction and therefore prohibits overlapping execution of another FPA instruction. (Note that load and store operations *can* be overlapped with these cycles.) Those instruction cycles that are lightly shaded ▨, however, are placing minimal demands on the FPA resources, and other instructions can be overlapped (with some restrictions) to obtain simultaneous execution of instructions without stalling the instruction pipeline.

For example, an instruction such as **DIV.D** that requires a large number of cycles to complete could begin execution, and another instruction such as **ADD.D** could be initiated and completed while the **DIV.D** instruction is still being executed. Note that only one multiply instruction can be running at a time and only one divide instruction can run at a time.

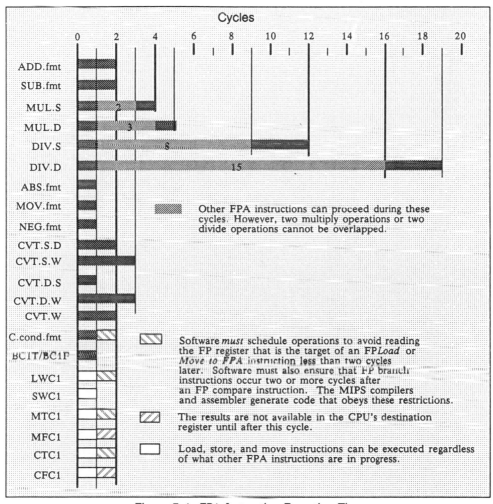

Figure 7.4 FPA Instruction Execution Times

Overlapping FPA Instructions

Figure 7.5 illustrates the overlapping of several FPA (and non–FPA) instructions. In this figure, the first instruction (**DIV.S**) requires a total of 12 cycles for execution but only the first cycle and last three cycles preclude the simultaneous execution of other FPA instructions. Similarly, the second instruction (**MUL.S**) has 2 cycles in the middle of its total of 4 required cycles that can be used to advance the execution of the third (**ADD.S**) and fourth instructions shown in the figure.

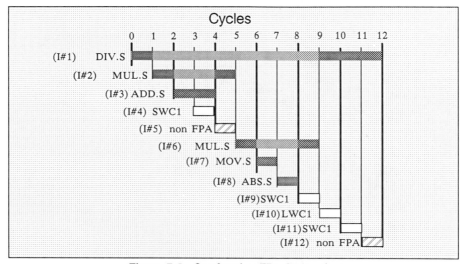

Figure 7.5 Overlapping FPA Instructions

Note that although processing of a single instruction consists of six pipe stages, the FPA does not require that an instruction actually be completed within six cycles to avoid stalling the instruction pipeline. If a subsequent instruction does not require FPA resources being used by a preceding instruction and has no data dependencies on preceding uncompleted instructions, then execution continues.

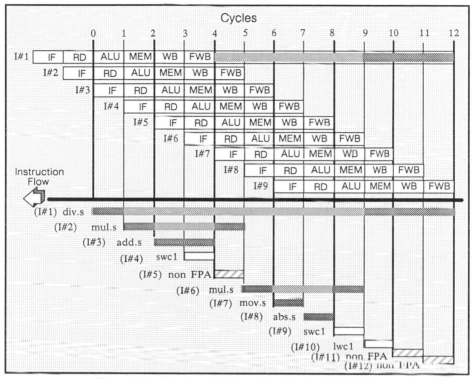

Figure 7.6 Overlapped Instructions in the FPA Pipeline

Figure 7.6 illustrates the progression of the FPA instruction pipeline with some over-lapped FPA instructions. The first instruction (**DIV.S**) in this figure requires eight additional cycles beyond its FWB pipe stage before it is completed. The pipeline need not be stalled, however, because the way in which the FPA instructions are overlapped avoids resource conflicts.

Figure 7.6 also presumes that there are no data dependencies between the instruc-tions that would stall the pipeline. For example, if any instruction before I#13 required the results of the **DIV.S** (I#1) instruction, then the pipeline would be stalled until those results were available.

8
Floating Point Exceptions

This chapter describes how the R2010 FPA handles floating point exceptions. A floating point exception occurs whenever the FPA cannot handle the operands or results of a floating point operation in the normal way. The FPA responds either by generating an interrupt to initiate a software trap or by setting a status flag. The Control/Status register described in **Chapter 6** contains a *trap enable* bit for each exception type that determines whether an exception will cause the FPA to initiate a trap or just set a status flag. If a trap is taken, the FPA remains in the state found at the beginning of the operation, and a software exception handling routine is executed. If no trap is taken, an appropriate value is written into the FPA destination register and execution continues.

The FPA supports the five IEEE exceptions -- inexact (I), overflow (O), underflow (U), divide by zero (Z), and invalid operation (V) -- with exception bits, trap enables, and sticky bits (status flags). The FPA adds a sixth exception type, unimplemented operation (E), to be used in those cases where the FPA itself cannot implement the standard MIPS floating-point architecture, including cases where the FPA cannot determine the correct exception behavior. This exception indicates that a software implementation must be used. The unimplemented operation exception has no trap enable or sticky bit; whenever this exception occurs, an unimplemented exception trap is taken (if the FPA's interrupt input to the R2000 is enabled).

Figure 8.1 illustrates the Control/Status register bits used to support exceptions.

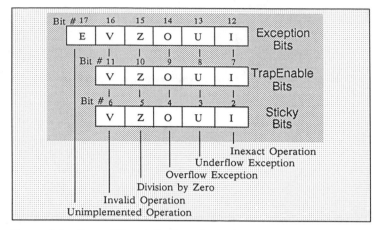

Figure 8.1   Control/Status Register Exception/Sticky/TrapEnable Bits

Each of the five IEEE exceptions (V, Z, O, U, I) is associated with a trap under user control which is enabled by setting one of the five *TrapEnable* bits. When an exception occurs, both the corresponding *Exception* and *Sticky* bits are set. If the corresponding *TrapEnable* bit is set, the FPA generates an interrupt to the R2000 processor and the subsequent exception processing allows a trap to be taken.

Exception Trap Processing

When a floating-point exception trap is taken, the R2000 Processor's Cause register (described in **Chapter 5**) indicates that an external interrupt from the FPA is the cause of the exception and the R2000's EPC (Exception Program Counter) contains the address of the instruction that caused the exception trap.

For each IEEE standard exception, a status flag (*Sticky* bit) is provided that is set on any occurrence of the corresponding exception condition with no corresponding exception trap signaled. The *Sticky* bits may be reset by writing a new value into the Control/Status register and may be saved and restored individually, or as a group, by software.

When no exception trap is signaled, a default action is taken by the FPA, which provides a substitute value for the original, exceptional, result of the floating-point operation. The default action taken depends on the type of exception, and in the case of the Overflow exception, the current rounding mode. Table 8.1 lists the default action taken by the FPA for each of the IEEE exceptions.

	Exception	Rounding Mode	Default Action (no exception trap signaled)
V	Invalid Operation	--	Supply a quiet NaN.
Z	Division by zero	--	Supply a properly signed ∞.
O	Overflow	RN	Modify overflow values to ∞ with the sign of the intermediate result.
		RZ	Modify overflow values to the format's largest finite number with the sign of the intermediate result.
		RP	Modify negative overflows to the format's most negative finite number. Modify positive overflows to + ∞.
		RM	Modify positive overflows to the format's largest finite number. Modify negative overflows to − ∞.
U	Underflow	--	Generate an Unimplemented exception.
I	Inexact	--	Supply a rounded result.

Table 8.1 FPA Exception Default Actions

The FPA internally detects eight different conditions that can cause exceptions. When the FPA encounters one of these unusual situations, it will cause either an IEEE exception or an Unimplemented Operation exception (E). Table 8.2 lists the exception–causing situations and contrasts the behavior of the FPA with the IEEE standard's requirements.

FPA internal result	IEEE Stndrd	Trap Enab.	Trap Disab.	Note
Inexact result	I	I	I	loss of accuracy
Exponent overflow	O I*	O I	O I	normalized exponent > Emax
Divide by zero	Z	Z	Z	zero is (exponent = Emin−1, mantissa = 0)
Overflow on convert	V	V	E	source out of integer range
Signaling NaN source	V	V	E	quiet NaN source produces quiet NaN result
Invalid operation	V	V	E	0/0 etc.
Exponent underflow	U	E	E	normalized exponent < Emin
Denormalized source	none	E	E	exponent = Emin−1 and mantissa<>0
* Standard specifies inexact exception on overflow only if overflow trap is disabled.				

Table 8.2 FPA Exception–causing Conditions

The sections that follow describe the conditions that cause the FPA to generate each of its six exceptions and details the FPA's response to each of these exception–causing situations.

Inexact Exception (I)

The FPA generates this exception if the rounded result of an operation is not exact or if it overflows.

NOTE: The FPA usually examines the operands of floating point operations before execution actually begins to determine (based on the exponent values of the operands) if the operation can *possibly* cause an exception. If there is a possibility of an instruction causing an exception trap, then the FPA uses a coprocessor stall mechanism to execute the instruction. It is impossible, however, for the FPA to predetermine if an instruction will produce an inexact result. Therefore, if inexact exception traps are enabled, the FPA uses the coprocessor stall mechanism to execute **all** floating point operations that require more than one cycle. Since this mode of execution can impact performance, inexact exception traps should be enabled only when necessary.

Trap Enabled Results: If inexact exception traps are enabled, the result register is not modified and the source registers are preserved.

Trap Disabled Results: The rounded or overflowed result is delivered to the destination register if no other software trap occurs.

Invalid Operation Exception (V)

The invalid operation exception is signaled if one or both of the operands are invalid for an implemented operation. The invalid operations are:

1) Addition or subtraction: magnitude subtraction of infinities, such as:
   $(+ \infty) - (+ \infty)$

2) Multiplication: 0 times ∞, with any signs

3) Division: $0 \div 0$, or $\infty \div \infty$, with any signs

4) Conversion of a floating-point number to a fixed-point format when an overflow, or operand value of infinity or NaN, precludes a faithful representation in that format

5) Comparison of predicates involving < or > without ?, when the operands are "unordered"

6) Any arithmetic operation on a signaling NaN. Note that a move (MOV) operation is not considered to be an arithmetic operation, but that ABS and NEG are considered to be arithmetic operations and will cause this exception if one or both operands is a signaling NaN.

Software may simulate this exception for other operations that are invalid for the given source operands. Examples of these operations include IEEE-specified functions implemented in software, such as Remainder: x REM y, where y is zero or x is infinite; conversion of a floating-point number to a decimal format whose value causes an overflow or is infinity or NaN; and transcendental functions, such as ln (-5) or $\cos^{-1}(3)$. Refer to **Appendix B** for examples or routines to handle these cases.

Trap Enabled Results: The original operand values are undisturbed.

Trap Disabled Results: The FPA always signals an Unimplemented exception because it does not create the NaN that the Standard specifies should be returned under these circumstances.

Division–by–Zero Exception (Z)

The division by zero exception is signaled on a divide operation if the divisor is zero and the dividend is a finite non–zero number.

Trap Enabled Results: The result register is not modified, and the source registers are preserved.

Trap Disabled Results: The result, when no trap occurs, is a correctly signed infinity.

Overflow Exception (O)

The overflow exception is signaled when what would have been the magnitude of the rounded floating–point result, were the exponent range unbounded, is larger than the destination format's largest finite number. (This exception also sets the Inexact exception and sticky bits.)

Trap Enabled Results: The result register is not modified, and the source registers are preserved.

Trap Disabled Results: The result, when no trap occurs, is determined by the rounding mode and the sign of the intermediate result (as listed in Table 8.1).

Underflow Exception (U)

The FPA never generates an Underflow exception and never sets the U bit in either the *Exceptions* field or *Sticky* field of the Control/Status register. If the FPA detects a condition that could be either an underflow or a loss of accuracy, it generates an Unimplemented exception.

Unimplemented Operation Exception (E)

The FPA generates this exception when it attempts to execute an instruction with an OpCode (bits 31–26) or format code (bits 24–21) which has been reserved for future use.

This exception is not maskable: the trap is always enabled. When an Unimplemented Operation is signaled, an interrupt is sent to the R2000 Processor so that the operation can be emulated in software. When the operation is emulated in software, any of the IEEE exceptions may arise; these exceptions must, in turn, be simulated.

This exception is also generated when any of the following exceptions are detected by the FPA:

- Denormalized Operand
- Not–a–Number (NaN) Operand
- Invalid operation with trap disabled
- Denormalized Result
- Underflow

Trap Enabled Results: The original operand values are undisturbed.

Trap Disabled Results: This trap cannot not be disabled.

Saving and Restoring State

Thirty–two coprocessor load or store instructions will save or restore the FPA's floating–point register state in memory. The contents of the Control/Status register can be saved using the "move to/from coprocessor control register" instructions (CTC1/CFC1). Normally, the Control/Status register contents are saved first and restored last.

If the Control/Status register is read when the coprocessor is executing one or more floating–point instructions, the instructions in progress (in the pipeline) are completed before the contents of the register are moved to the main processor. If an exception occurs during one of the in–progress instructions, that exception is written into the Control/Status register *Exceptions* field.

Note that the *Exceptions* field of the Control/Status register holds the results of only one instruction: the FPA examines source operands before an operation is initiated to determine if the instruction can possibly cause an exception. If an exception is possible, the FPA executes the instruction in "stall" mode to ensure that no more than one instruction at a time is executed that might cause an exception.

All of the bits in the *Exceptions* field can be cleared by writing a zero value to this field. This permits restarting of normal processing after the Control/Status register state is restored.

A

R2000 Processor
Instruction Set Details

This appendix provides a detailed description of the operation of each R2000 instruction. The instructions are listed in alphabetical order.

Refer to **Appendix B** for a detailed description of the R2010 FPA instructions.

The exceptions that may occur due to the execution of each instruction are listed after the description of each instruction. The description of the immediate causes and manner of handling exceptions is omitted from the instruction descriptions in this chapter. Refer to **Chapter 5** for detailed descriptions of exceptions and handling.

A chart on the last page of this appendix lists the bit encoding for the constant fields of each instruction.

Instruction Classes

R2000 instructions are divided into the following classes:

- **Load/Store** instructions move data between memory and general registers. They are all I–type instructions, since the only addressing mode
  supported is *base register + 16–bit immediate offset*.

- **Computational** instructions perform arithmetic, logical and shift operations on values in registers. They occur in both R–type (both operands are registers) and I–type (one operand is a 16–bit immediate)
  formats.

- **Jump** and **Branch** instructions change the control flow of a program.
  Jumps are always to absolute 26–bit word addresses (J–type format),
  or 32–bit register addresses (R–type). Branches have 16–bit offsets
  relative to the program counter (I–type). Jump and Link instructions
  save a return address in Register 31.

- **Coprocessor** instructions perform operations in the coprocessors.
  Coprocessor Loads and Stores are I–type. Coprocessor computational
  instructions have coprocessor–dependent formats (see the FPA instructions). Coprocessor zero (CP0) instructions manipulate the memory management and exception handling facilities of the processor.

- **Special** instructions perform a variety of tasks, including movement of
  data between special and general registers, syscall, and breakpoint.
  They are always R–type.

Instruction Formats

Every R2000 instruction consists of a single word (32 bits) aligned on a word boundary and there are only three instruction formats as shown in Figure A.1.

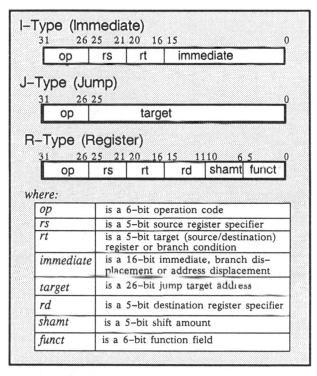

Figure A.1 R2000 Instruction Formats

Instruction Notation Conventions

In this appendix, all variable subfields in an instruction format (such as *rs*, *rt*, *immediate*, etc.) are shown in lower-case names.

For the sake of clarity, we sometimes use an alias for a variable subfield in the formats of specific instructions. For example, we use *rs = base* in the format for Load and Store instructions. Such an alias is always lower case, since it refers to a variable subfield.

In the instruction descriptions that follow, the *Operation* section describes the operation performed by each instruction using a high–level language notation. Special symbols used in the notation are described in Table A.2.

Symbol	Meaning
←	Assignment
‖	Bit string concatenation
x^y	Replication of bit value x into a y–bit string. Note that x is always a single–bit value.
$x_{y..z}$	Selection of bits y through z of bit string x. Little–endian bit notation is always used. If y is less than z, this expression is an empty (zero length) bit string.
+	Two's complement addition
−	Two's complement subtraction
∗	Two's complement multiplication
div	Two's complement integer division
mod	Two's complement modulo
<	Two's complement less than comparison
and	Bitwise logic AND
or	Bitwise logic OR
xor	Bitwise logic XOR
nor	Bitwise logic NOR
GPR[x]	General Register x. The contents of GPR[0] is always zero. Attempts to alter the contents of GPR[0] have no effect.
CPR[z,x]	Coprocessor unit z, general register x
CCR[z,x]	Coprocessor unit z, control register x
T+ i	Indicates the time steps (CPU cycles) between operations. Thus, operations identified as occurring at T+1 are performed during the cycle following the one where the instruction was initiated. This type of operation occurs with loads, stores, jumps, branches and coprocessor instructions.
vAddress	Virtual address
pAddress	Physical address

Table A.2   R2000 Instruction Operation Notations

Instruction Notation Examples

The following examples illustrate the application of some of the instruction notation conventions:

Example #1:

$$GPR[rt] \leftarrow Immediate \parallel 0^{16}$$

Sixteen zero bits are concatenated with an immediate value (typically 16 bits), and the 32-bit string (with the lower 16 bits set to zero) is assigned to General Purpose Register *rt*.

Example #2:

$$(immediate_{15})^{16} \parallel immediate_{15..0}$$

Bit 15 (the sign bit) of an immediate value is extended for 16 bit positions, and the result is concatenated with bits 15 through 0 of the immediate value to form a 32-bit sign-extended value.

Load and Store Instructions

All load operations have a latency of one instruction. That is, the instruction immediately following a load cannot use the contents of the register which will be loaded with the data being fetched from storage. An exception is that the target register for the load word left and load word right instructions may be specified as the same register used as the destination of a load instruction that immediately precedes it.

In the load/store operation descriptions, the functions listed in Table A.2a are used to summarize the handling of virtual addresses and physical memory.

Function	Description
Addr Translation	Uses the TLB to find the physical address given the virtual address. The function fails and an exception is taken if the entry for the page containing the virtual address is not present in the TLB (Translation Lookaside Buffer).
Load Memory	Uses the cache and main memory to find the contents of the word containing the specified physical address. The low-order two bits of the address and the access type field indicate which of each of the four bytes within the data word need to be returned. If the cache is enabled for this access, the entire word is returned and loaded into the cache.
Store Memory	Uses the cache, write buffer, and main memory to store the word or part of word specified as data into the word containing the specified physical address. The low-order two bits of the address and the access type field indicate which of the four bytes within the data word should be stored.

Table A.2a   Load/Store Common Functions

The access type field indicates the size of the data item to be loaded or stored as shown in Table A.2b. Regardless of access type or byte-numbering order (endianness), the address specifies the byte which has the smallest byte address of the bytes in the addressed field. For a big-endian machine, this is the leftmost byte and contains the sign for a two's complement number; for a little-endian machine, this is the rightmost byte and contains the lowest precision byte.

Access Type		Meaning
Mnemonic	Value	
WORD	3	word (32 bits)
TRIPLE-BYTE	2	triple-byte (24 bits)
HALFWORD	1	halfword (16 bits)
BYTE	0	byte (8 bits)

Table A.2b   Access Type Specifications for Loads/Stores

The bytes within the addressed word which are used can be determined directly from the access type and the two low-order bits of the address, as shown in Table A.2c. Note that certain combinations of access type and low-order address bits can never occur (WORD/01/10/11, TRIPLE-BYTE/10/11, HALFWORD/01/11).

Access Type 1 0	Low-Order Address Bits 1 0	Bytes Accessed								
		31 ——— Big-Endian ——— 0				31 ——— Little-Endian ——— 0				
1 1 (word)	0 0	0	1	2	3	3	2	1	0	
1 0 (triple-byte)	0 0	0	1	2			2	1	0	
	0 1		1	2	3	3	2	1		
0 1 (halfword)	0 0	0	1					1	0	
	1 0			2	3	3	2			
0 0 (byte)	0 0	0							0	
	0 1		1					1		
	1 0			2			2			
	1 1				3	3				

Table A.2c Byte Specifications for Loads/Stores

Jump and Branch Instructions

All jump and branch instructions are implemented with a delay of exactly one instruction. That is, the instruction immediately following a jump or branch (i.e., occupying the delay slot) is always executed while the target instruction is being fetched from storage. It is not valid for a delay slot to be occupied itself by a jump or branch instruction; however, this error is not detected, and the results of such an operation are undefined.

If an exception or interrupt prevents the completion of a legal instruction during a delay slot, the R2000 sets the EPC register to point at the jump or branch instruction which precedes it. When the code is restarted, both the jump or branch instructions and the instruction in the delay slot are re-executed.

Because jump and branch instructions may be restarted after exceptions or interrupts, they must be restartable. Therefore, when a jump or branch instruction stores a return link value, register 31 may not be used as a source register.

Since instructions must be word-aligned, a *Jump Register* or *Jump and Link Register* instruction must use a register whose two low-order bits are zero. If these low order bits are not zero, an address exception will occur when the jump target instruction is subsequently fetched.

Coprocessor Instructions

The MIPS architecture provides four coprocessor units, or classes. Coprocessors are alternate execution units, which have separate register files from the R2000 processor. Each coprocessor has 2 register spaces, each with thirty–two 32–bit registers. The first space, *coprocessor general registers,* may be directly loaded from memory and stored into memory, and their contents may be transferred between the coprocessor and processor. The second, *coprocessor control registers,* may only have their contents transferred directly between the coprocessor and processor. Coprocessor instructions may alter registers in either space.

Normally, by convention, coprocessor control register 0 is interpreted as a coprocessor revision register. However, the system control coprocessor (CP0) uses coprocessor general register 15 for the processor/coprocessor revision register. The register's low–order byte (bits 7..0) is interpreted as a coprocessor unit implementation descriptor. The second byte (bits 15..8) is interpreted as a coprocessor unit revision number. The contents of the high–order halfword of the register are not defined.

System Control Coprocessor (CP0) Instructions

There are some special limitations imposed on operations involving the System Control Coprocessor (CP0) that is incorporated within the R2000. Although load and store instructions to transfer data to and from coprocessors and move control to/from coprocessor instructions are generally permitted by the R2000 architecture, CP0 is given a somewhat protected status since it has responsibility for exception handling and memory management. Therefore, the move to/from coprocessor instructions are the only valid mechanism for reading from and writing to the CP0 registers.

Several coprocessor operation instructions are defined for CP0 to directly read, write, and probe TLB entries and to modify the operating modes in preparation for returning to user–mode or interrupt–enabled states.

ADD

ADD

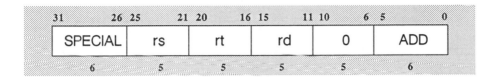

Format:

ADD rd,rs,rt

Description:

The contents of general register *rs* and the contents of general register *rt* are added to form a 32–bit result. The result is placed into general register *rd*.

An overflow exception occurs if the two highest order carry–out bits differ (two's complement overflow).

Operation:

T:	GPR[rd] ← GPR[rs] + GPR[rt]

Exceptions:

Overflow exception

ADDI

Add Immediate

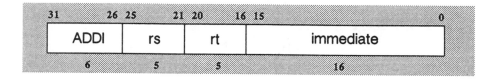

Format:

ADDI rt,rs,immediate

Description:

The 16–bit *immediate* is sign–extended and added to the contents of general register *rs* to form a 32–bit result. The result is placed into general register *rt*.

An overflow exception occurs if the two highest order carry–out bits differ (two's complement overflow).

Operation:

$$T: \quad GPR[rt] \leftarrow GPR[rs] + (immediate_{15})^{16} \parallel immediate_{15..0}$$

Exceptions:

Overflow exception

Add Immediate Unsigned   ADDIU

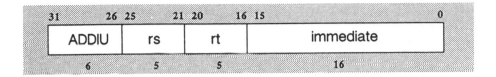

Format:

ADDIU rt,rs,immediate

Description:

The 16-bit *immediate* is sign-extended and added to the contents of general register *rs* to form a 32-bit result. The result is placed into general register *rt*. No overflow exception occurs under any circumstances.

Note that the only difference between this instruction and the ADDI instruction is that ADDIU never causes an overflow exception.

Operation:

$$T: \qquad GPR[rt] \leftarrow GPR[rs] + (immediate_{15})^{16} \parallel immediate_{15..0}$$

Exceptions:

None.

ADDU

ADD Unsigned

31 26	25 21	20 16	15 11	10 6	5 0
SPECIAL	rs	rt	rd	0	ADDU
6	5	5	5	5	6

Format:

ADDU rd,rs,rt

Description:

The contents of general register *rs* and the contents of general register *rt* are added to form a 32–bit result. The result is placed into general register *rd*.

No overflow exception occurs under any circumstances.

Note that the only difference between this instruction and the ADD instruction is that ADDU never causes an overflow exception.

Operation:

T: GPR[rd] ← GPR[rs] + GPR[rt]

Exceptions:

None.

And

AND

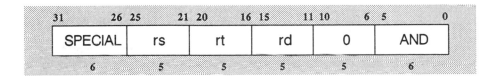

Format:

AND rd,rs,rt

Description:

The contents of general register *rs* are combined with the contents of general register *rt* in a bit–wise logical AND operation. The result is placed into general register *rd*.

Operation:

T:	GPR[rd] ← GPR[rs] *and* GPR[rt]

Exceptions:

None.

ANDI

And Immediate

31	26	25	21	20	16	15		0
ANDI		rs		rt		immediate		
6		5		5		16		

Format:

ANDI rt,rs,immediate

Description:

The 16–bit *immediate* is zero–extended and combined with the contents of general register *rs* in a bit–wise logical AND operation. The result is placed into general register *rt*.

Operation:

$$T: \quad GPR[rt] \leftarrow 0^{16} \parallel (immediate \; and \; GPR[rs]_{15..0})$$

Exceptions:

None.

Branch On Coprocessor z False   **BCzF**

31 26	25 16	15 0
COPz	BCF	offset
6	10	16

Format:

BCzF   offset

Description:

A branch target address is computed from the sum of the address of the instruction in the delay slot and the 16-bit *offset*, shifted left two bits and sign-extended to 32 bits. If the coprocessor z's condition signal (CpCond) is false, then the program branches to the target address, with a delay of one instruction.

Operation:

$$T: \quad target \leftarrow (offset_{15})^{14} \parallel offset \parallel 0^2$$
$$condition \leftarrow not\ CpCond[z]$$
$$T+1: \quad if\ condition\ then$$
$$PC \leftarrow PC + target$$
$$endif$$

Exceptions:

Coprocessor unusable exception

BCzT

Branch On Coprocessor z True

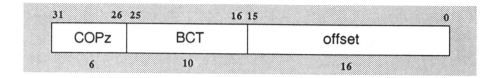

Format:

BCzT   offset

Description:

A branch target address is computed from the sum of the address of the instruction in the delay slot and the 16-bit *offset*, shifted left two bits and sign-extended to 32 bits. If the coprocessor *z*'s condition signal (CpCond) is true, then the program branches to the target address, with a delay of one instruction.

Operation:

$$
\begin{array}{ll}
\text{T:} & \text{target} \leftarrow (\text{offset}_{15})^{14} \parallel \text{offset} \parallel 0^2 \\
 & \text{condition} \leftarrow \text{CpCond}[z] \\
\text{T+1:} & \text{if condition then} \\
 & \qquad \text{PC} \leftarrow \text{PC + target} \\
 & \quad \text{endif}
\end{array}
$$

Exceptions:

Coprocessor unusable exception

Branch On Equal

BEQ

31 26	25 21	20 16	15 0
BEQ	rs	rt	offset
6	5	5	16

Format:

BEQ rs,rt,offset

Description:

A branch target address is computed from the sum of the address of the instruction in the delay slot and the 16-bit *offset*, shifted left two bits and sign-extended to 32 bits. The contents of general register *rs* and the contents of general register *rt* are compared. If the two registers are equal, then the program branches to the target address, with a delay of one instruction.

Operation:

$$\text{T:} \quad \text{target} \leftarrow (\text{offset}_{15})^{14} \parallel \text{offset} \parallel 0^2$$

$$\text{condition} \leftarrow (\text{GPR[rs]} = \text{GPR[rt]})$$

$$\text{T+1:} \quad \text{if condition then}$$
$$\text{PC} \leftarrow \text{PC} + \text{target}$$
$$\text{endif}$$

Exceptions:

None.

BGEZ

**Branch On Greater
Than Or Equal To Zero**

31　　　　26	25　　　21	20　　　16	15　　　　　　　　0
BCOND	rs	BGEZ	offset
6	5	5	16

Format:

BGEZ   rs,offset

Description:

A branch target address is computed from the sum of the address of the instruction in the delay slot and the 16–bit *offset*, shifted left two bits and sign–extended to 32 bits. If the contents of general register *rs* have the sign bit cleared, then the program branches to the target address, with a delay of one instruction.

Operation:

$$T:\quad target \leftarrow (offset_{15})^{14} \parallel offset \parallel 0^2$$
$$condition \leftarrow (GPR[rs]_{31} = 0)$$
$$T+1:\quad \text{if condition then}$$
$$PC \leftarrow PC + target$$
$$\text{endif}$$

Exceptions:

None.

Branch On Greater Than Or Equal To Zero And Link

BGEZAL

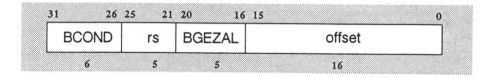

Format:

BGEZAL rs,offset

Description:

A branch target address is computed from the sum of the address of the instruction in the delay slot and the 16-bit *offset,* shifted left two bits and sign-extended to 32 bits. Unconditionally, the address of the instruction after the delay slot is placed in the link register, r31. If the contents of general register *rs* have the sign bit cleared, then the program branches to the target address, with a delay of one instruction.

General register *rs* may not be general register 31, because such an instruction is not restartable. An attempt to execute this instruction is *not* trapped, however.

Operation:

$$
\begin{aligned}
\text{T:} \quad & \text{target} \leftarrow (\text{offset}_{15})^{14} \,\|\, \text{offset} \,\|\, 0^2 \\
& \text{condition} \leftarrow (\text{GPR[rs]}_{31} = 0) \\
& \text{GPR[31]} \leftarrow \text{PC} + 8 \\
\text{T + 1:} \quad & \text{if condition then} \\
& \quad \text{PC} \leftarrow \text{PC} + \text{target} \\
& \quad \text{endif}
\end{aligned}
$$

Exceptions:

None.

BGTZ

**Branch On Greater
Than Zero**

31 26	25 21	20 16	15 0
BGTZ	rs	0	offset
6	5	5	16

Format:

BGTZ rs,offset

Description:

A branch target address is computed from the sum of the address of the instruction in the delay slot and the 16-bit *offset*, shifted left two bits and sign-extended to 32 bits. The contents of general register *rs* are compared to zero. If the contents of general register *rs* have the sign bit cleared and are not equal to zero, then the program branches to the target address, with a delay of one instruction.

Operation:

$$T: \quad target \leftarrow (offset_{15})^{14} \parallel offset \parallel 0^2$$
$$condition \leftarrow (GPR[rs]_{31} = 0) \text{ and } (GPR[rs] \neq GPR[r0])$$
$$T + 1: \quad \text{if condition then}$$
$$PC \leftarrow PC + target$$
$$\text{endif}$$

Exceptions:

None.

Branch on Less Than Or Equal To Zero

BLEZ

31 26	25 21	20 16	15 0
BLEZ	rs	0	offset
6	5	5	16

Format:

BLEZ   rs,offset

Description:

A branch target address is computed from the sum of the address of the instruction in the delay slot and the 16–bit *offset*, shifted left two bits and sign–extended to 32 bits. The contents of general register *rs* is compared to zero. If the contents of general register *rs* have the sign bit sct, or are equal to zero, then the program branches to the target address, with a delay of one instruction.

Operation:

$$T: \quad target \leftarrow (offset_{15})^{14} \, \| \, offset \, \| \, 0^2$$
$$condition \leftarrow (GPR[rs]_{31} = 1) \text{ or } (GPR[rs] = GPR[r0])$$
$$T + 1: \quad \text{if condition then}$$
$$PC \leftarrow PC + target$$
$$\text{endif}$$

Exceptions:

None.

BLTZ

Branch On Less Than Zero

31	26	25	21	20	16	15	0
BCOND		rs		BLTZ		offset	
6		5		5		16	

Format:

BLTZ rs,offset

Description:

A branch target address is computed from the sum of the address of the instruction in the delay slot and the 16–bit *offset*, shifted left two bits and sign–extended to 32 bits. If the contents of general register *rs* have the sign bit set, then the program branches to the target address, with a delay of one instruction.

Operation:

$$
\begin{array}{ll}
\text{T:} & \text{target} \leftarrow (\text{offset}_{15})^{14} \parallel \text{offset} \parallel 0^2 \\
& \text{condition} \leftarrow (\text{GPR[rs]}_{31} = 1) \\
\text{T + 1:} & \text{if condition then} \\
& \qquad \text{PC} \leftarrow \text{PC + target} \\
& \qquad \text{endif}
\end{array}
$$

Exceptions:

None.

Branch On Less
Than Zero And Link

BLTZAL

BCOND	rs	BLTZAL	offset
6	5	5	16

31   26 25   21 20   16 15   0

Format:

BLTZAL rs,offset

Description:

A branch target address is computed from the sum of the address of the instruction in the delay slot and the 16–bit *offset,* shifted left two bits and sign–extended to 32 bits. Unconditionally, the address of the instruction after the delay slot is placed in the link register, r31. If the contents of general register *rs* have the sign bit set, then the program branches to the target address, with a delay of one instruction.

General register *rs* may not be general register 31, because such an instruction is not restartable. An attempt to execute this instruction is *not* trapped, however.

Operation:

$$
\begin{aligned}
\text{T:}\quad & \text{target} \leftarrow (\text{offset}_{15})^{14} \,\|\, \text{offset} \,\|\, 0^2 \\
& \text{condition} \leftarrow (\text{GPR[rs]}_{31} = 1) \\
& \text{GPR[31]} \leftarrow \text{PC} + 8 \\
\text{T + 1:}\quad & \text{if condition then} \\
& \quad \text{PC} \leftarrow \text{PC} + \text{target} \\
& \quad \text{endif}
\end{aligned}
$$

Exceptions:

None.

BNE

Branch On Not Equal

31 26	25 21	20 16	15 0
BNE	rs	rt	offset
6	5	5	16

Format:

BNE   rs,rt,offset

Description:

A branch target address is computed from the sum of the address of the instruction in the delay slot and the 16–bit *offset,* shifted left two bits and sign–extended to 32 bits. The contents of general register *rs* and the contents of general register *rt* are compared. If the two registers are not equal, then the program branches to the target address, with a delay of one instruction.

Operation:

$$
\begin{aligned}
\text{T:} \quad & \text{target} \leftarrow (\text{offset}_{15})^{14} \,\|\, \text{offset} \,\|\, 0^2 \\
& \text{condition} \leftarrow (\text{GPR[rs]} \neq \text{GPR[rt]}) \\
\text{T + 1:} \quad & \text{if condition then} \\
& \qquad \text{PC} \leftarrow \text{PC + target} \\
& \qquad \text{endif}
\end{aligned}
$$

Exceptions:

None.

Break   BREAK

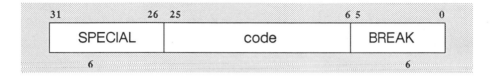

Format:

BREAK

Description:

A breakpoint trap occurs, immediately and unconditionally transferring control to the exception handler.

The code field is available for use as software parameters, but is retrieved by the exception handler only by loading the contents of the memory word containing the instruction.

Operation:

PC ← ExceptionHandler

Exceptions:

Breakpoint trap

CFCz

Move Control From
Coprocessor

31	26 25	21 20	16 15	11 10	0
COPz	CF	rt	rd	0	
6	5	5	5	11	

Format:

CFCz   rt,rd

Description:

The contents of coprocessor control register *rd* of coprocessor unit z are loaded into general register *rt*.

Operation:

```
T:   data  ←  CCR[z,rd]

T + 1: GPR[rt]  ←  data
```

Exceptions:

Coprocessor unusable exception

Coprocessor Operation   COPz

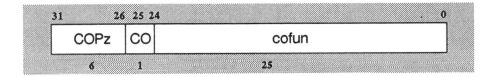

Format:

COPz   cofun

Description:

A coprocessor operation is performed. The operation may specify and reference internal coprocessor registers, and may change the state of the coprocessor condition line, but does not modify state within the processor or the cache/memory system.

Operation:

```
T:   CoprocessorOperation (z, cofun)
```

Exceptions:

Coprocessor unusable exception

CTCz

Move Control to Coprocessor

31 26	25 21	20 16	15 11	10 0
COPz	CT	rt	rd	0
6	5	5	5	11

Format:

CTCz   rt,rd

Description:

The contents of general register *rt* are loaded into control register *rd* of coprocessor unit z.

Operation:

```
T:   data   ←  GPR[rt]
T + 1: CCR[z,rd]  ←  data
```

Exceptions:

Coprocessor unusable exception

Divide

DIV

31 26	25 21	20 16	15 6	5 0
SPECIAL	rs	rt	0	DIV
6	5	5	10	6

Format:

DIV rs,rt

Description:

The contents of general register *rs* are divided by the contents of general register *rt*, treating both operands as 32–bit two's complement values.   No overflow exception occurs under any circumstances.

When the operation completes, the quotient word of the double result is loaded into special register LO, and the remainder word of the double result is loaded into special register HI. The MFHI and MFLO instructions are interlocked so that any attempt to read them before operations have completed will cause execution of instructions to be delayed until the operation finishes.

Divide operations are performed by a separate, autonomous execution unit within the R2000. After a divide operation is started, execution of other instructions may continue in parallel. The multiply/divide unit continues to operate during cache miss and other delaying cycles in which no instructions are executed.

Operation:

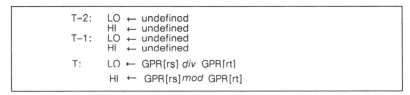

```
T-2:   LO ← undefined
       HI ← undefined
T-1:   LO ← undefined
       HI ← undefined
T:     LO ← GPR[rs] div GPR[rt]
       HI ← GPR[rs] mod GPR[rt]
```

Exceptions:

None.

DIVU

Divide Unsigned

31 26	25 21	20 16	15 6	5 0
SPECIAL	rs	rt	0	DIVU
6	5	5	10	6

Format:

DIVU rs,rt

Description:

The contents of general register *rs* are divided by the contents of general register *rt*, treating both operands as 32-bit two's unsigned values. No overflow exception occurs under any circumstances.

When the operation completes, the quotient word of the double result is loaded into special register LO, and the remainder word of the double result is loaded into special register HI. The MFHI and MFLO instructions are interlocked so that any attempt to read them before operations have completed will cause execution of instructions to be delayed until the operation finishes.

Divide operations are performed by a separate, autonomous execution unit within the R2000. After a divide operation is started, execution of other instructions may continue in parallel. The multiply/divide unit continues to operate during cache miss and other delaying cycles in which no instructions are executed.

Operation:

```
T-2:   LO ← undefined
       HI ← undefined
T-1:   LO ← undefined
       HI ← undefined

T:     LO ← (0 ‖ GPR[rs]) div (0 ‖ GPR[rt])
       HI ← (0 ‖ GPR[rs]) mod (0 ‖ GPR[rt])
```

Exceptions:

None.

Jump J

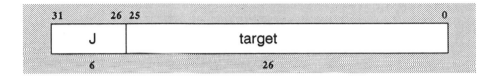

Format:

J target

Description:

The 26–bit target address is shifted left two bits, combined with the high order 4 bits of the current program counter, and the program unconditionally jumps to the calculated address, with a delay of one instruction.

Operation:

> T: $temp \leftarrow PC_{31..28} \parallel target \parallel 0^2$
> T+1: $PC \leftarrow temp$

Exceptions:

None.

JAL

Jump And Link

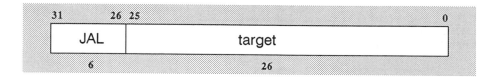

Format:

JAL   target

Description:

The 26–bit target address is shifted left two bits, combined with the high order 4 bits of the current program counter, and the program unconditionally jumps to the calculated address, with a delay of one instruction. The address of the instruction after the delay slot is placed in the link register, *r31*.

Operation:

$$
\begin{aligned}
&\text{T:} \quad temp \leftarrow PC_{31..28} \parallel target \parallel 0^2 \\
&\qquad GPR[31] \leftarrow PC + 8 \\
&\text{T+1:} \quad PC \leftarrow temp
\end{aligned}
$$

Exceptions:

None.

Jump And Link Register

JALR

31 26	25 21	20 16	15 11	10 6	5 0
SPECIAL	rs	0	rd	0	JALR
6	5	5	5	5	6

Format:

JALR rs
JALR rd, rs

Description:

The program unconditionally jumps to the address contained in general register *rs*, with a delay of one instruction. The address of the instruction after the delay slot is placed in general register *rd*.   The default value of *rd*, if omitted in the assembly language instruction, is 31.

Register specifiers *rs* and *rd* may not be equal, because such an instruction does not have the same effect when re-executed. However, an attempt to execute this instruction is *not* trapped; the result of executing such an instruction is undefined.

Operation:

```
T:    temp ← GPR[rs]
      GPR[rd] ← PC + 8
T+1:  PC ← temp
```

Exceptions:

None.

Since instructions must be word-aligned, a *Jump and Link Register* instruction must specify a target register (rs) whose two low-order bits are zero. If these low-order bits are not zero, an address exception will occur when the jump target instruction is subsequently fetched.

JR

Jump Register

31	26	25	21	20	6	5	0
SPECIAL		rs		0		JR	
6		5		15		6	

Format:

JR rs

Description:

The program unconditionally jumps to the address contained in general register *rs*, with a delay of one instruction.

Operation:

```
T:    temp ← GPR[rs]
T+1:  PC ← temp
```

Exceptions:

None.

Since instructions must be word–aligned, a *Jump Register* instruction must specify a target register (rs) whose two low–order bits are zero. If these low–order bits are not zero, an address exception will occur when the jump target instruction is subsequently fetched.

Load Byte

LB

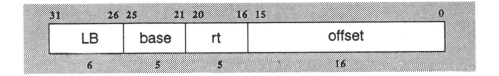

31	26	25	21	20	16	15		0
LB		base		rt			offset	
6		5		5			16	

Format:

LB rt,offset(base)

Description:

The 16–bit *offset* is sign–extended and added to the contents of general register *base* to form a 32–bit unsigned effective address. The contents of the byte at the memory location specified by the effective address are sign–extended and loaded into general register *rt*.

Operation:

T: vAddress← (offset $_{15}$) ^{16} ‖ offset $_{15..0}$ +GPR[base]
        (pAddress, nonCacheable) ← AddrTranslation (vAddress)
        mem←LoadMemory (nonCacheable, BYTE, pAddress)
        byte ←vAddress $_{1..0}$

T + 1: if BigEndian then
            GPR[rt] ← (mem $_{31-8 \cdot byte}$) ^{24} ‖ mem $_{31-8 \cdot byte .. 24-8 \cdot byte}$
        else
            GPR[rt] ← (mem $_{7+8 \cdot byte}$) ^{24} ‖ mem $_{7+8 \cdot byte . 8 \cdot byte}$
        endif

Exceptions:

UTLB miss fault
TLB miss fault
Bus error exception
Address error exception

LBU

Load Byte Unsigned

31	26	25	21	20	16	15	0
LBU		base		rt		offset	
6		5		5		16	

Format:

LBU rt,offset(base)

Description:

The 16–bit *offset* is sign–extended and added to the contents of general register *base* to form a 32–bit unsigned effective address. The contents of the byte at the memory location specified by the effective address are zero–extended and loaded into general register *rt*.

Operation:

T: vAddress← (offset $_{15}$) ^{16} ‖ offset $_{15..0}$ +GPR[base]
        (pAddress, nonCacheable) ← AddrTranslation (vAddress)
        mem ← LoadMemory (nonCacheable, BYTE, pAddress)
        byte ← vAddress$_{1..0}$

T + 1: if BigEndian then
           GPR[rt] ← 0^{24} ‖ mem$_{31-8 \cdot byte..24-8 \cdot byte}$
       else
           GPR[rt] ← 0^{24} ‖ mem$_{7+8 \cdot byte..8 \cdot byte}$
       endif

Exceptions:

UTLB miss fault
TLB miss fault
Bus error exception
Address error exception

Load Halfword

LH

31	26	25	21	20	16	15	0

LH	base	rt	offset
6	5	5	16

Format:

LH rt,offset(base)

Description:

The 16-bit *offset* is sign-extended and added to the contents of general register *base* to form a 32-bit unsigned effective address. The contents of the halfword at the memory location specified by the effective address are sign-extended and loaded into general register *rt*.

If the least significant bit of the effective address is non-zero, an address error exception occurs.

Operation:

T: $vAddress \leftarrow (offset_{15})^{16} \parallel offset_{15..0} + GPR[base]$
    $(pAddress, nonCacheable) \leftarrow AddrTranslation (vAddress)$
    $mem \leftarrow LoadMemory (nonCacheable, HALFWORD, pAddress)$
    $byte \leftarrow vAddress_{1..0}$

T + 1: if BigEndian then
        $GPR[rt] \leftarrow (mem_{31-8*byte})^{16} \parallel mem_{31-8*byte..16-8*byte}$
    else
        $GPR[rt] \leftarrow (mem_{15+8*byte})^{16} \parallel mom_{15+8*byte..8*byte}$
    endif

Exceptions:

UTLB miss fault
TLB miss fault
Bus error exception
Address error exception

LHU

Load Halfword Unsigned

31 26	25 21	20 16	15 0
LHU	base	rt	offset
6	5	5	16

Format:

LHU rt,offset(base)

Description:

The 16–bit *offset* is sign–extended and added to the contents of general register *base* to form a 32–bit unsigned effective address. The contents of the halfword at the memory location specified by the effective address are zero–extended and loaded into general register *rt*.

If the least significant bit of the effective address is non–zero, an address error exception occurs.

Operation:

T: vAddress $\leftarrow$ (offset $_{15}$) ^{16} $\|$ offset $_{15..0}$ +GPR[base]
        (pAddress, nonCacheable) $\leftarrow$ AddrTranslation (vAddress)
        mem $\leftarrow$ LoadMemory (nonCacheable, HALFWORD, pAddress)
        byte $\leftarrow$ vAddress $_{1..0}$

T + 1: if BigEndian then
            GPR[rt] $\leftarrow$ 0^{16} $\|$ mem$_{31-8*byte..16-8*byte}$
        else
            GPR[rt] $\leftarrow$ 0^{16} $\|$ mem$_{15+8*byte..8*byte}$
        endif

Exceptions:

UTLB miss fault
TLB miss fault
Bus error exception
Address error exception

Load Upper Immediate

LUI

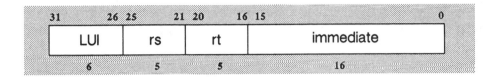

Format:

LUI   rt,immediate

Description:

The 16–bit *immediate* is shifted left 16 bits and concatenated to 16 bits of zeroes. The result is placed into general register *rt*.

Operation:

T·   GPR[rt] ← immediate $\|$ 0^{16}

Exceptions:

None.

LW

Load Word

31 26	25 21	20 16	15 0
LW	base	rt	offset
6	5	5	16

Format:

LW   rt,offset(base)

Description:

The 16–bit *offset* is sign–extended and added to the contents of general register *base* to form a 32–bit unsigned effective address. The contents of the word at the memory location specified by the effective address are loaded into general register *rt*.

If either of the two least significant bits of the effective address is non–zero, an address error exception occurs.

Operation:

```
T:      vAddress← (offset 15) 16 ‖ offset 15..0 +GPR[base]
        (pAddress, nonCacheable) ← AddrTranslation (vAddress)
        mem ← LoadMemory (nonCacheable, WORD, pAddress)
        byte ← vAddress 1..0
T+1:    GPR[rt] ← mem;
```

Exceptions:

UTLB miss fault
TLB miss fault
Bus error exception
Address error exception

Load Word To Coprocessor   LWCz

31	26 25	21 20	16 15	0
LWCz	base	rt	offset	
6	5	5	16	

Format:

LWCz rt,offset(base)

Description:

The 16-bit *offset* is sign-extended and added to the contents of general register *base* to form a 32-bit unsigned effective address. The contents of the word at the memory location specified by the effective address are loaded into coprocessor register *rt* of coprocessor unit z.

If either of the two least significant bits of the effective address is non-zero, an address error exception occurs.

Operation:

$$T: \quad vAddress \leftarrow (offset_{15})^{16} \parallel offset_{15..0} + GPR[base])$$
$$(pAddress, nonCacheable) \leftarrow AddrTranslation (vAddress)$$
$$mem \leftarrow LoadMemory (nonCacheable, WORD, pAddress_{31..2} \parallel 0^2$$
$$byte \leftarrow vAddress_{1..0}$$
$$T+1: \quad CPR[z,rt] \leftarrow mem;$$

Exceptions:

UTLB miss fault
TLB miss fault
Bus error exception
Address error exception
Coprocessor unusable exception

LWL
Load Word Left

31 26	25 21	20 16	15 0
LWL	base	rt	offset
6	5	5	16

Format:

LWL rt,offset(base)

Description:

This instruction can be used in combination with the LWR instruction to load a register with four consecutive bytes from memory, when the bytes cross a boundary between two words. LWL loads the left portion of the register from the appropriate part of the high–order word; LWR loads the right portion of the register from the appropriate part of the low–order word.

The LWL instruction adds its sign–extended 16–bit *offset* to the contents of general register *base* to form a 32–bit unsigned effective address which can specify an arbitrary byte. It reads bytes **only** from the word in memory which contains the specified starting byte. From one to four bytes will be loaded, depending on the starting byte specified.

Conceptually, it starts at the specified byte in memory and loads that byte into the high–order (left–most) byte of the register; then it proceeds toward the low–order byte of the word in memory and the low–order byte of the register, loading bytes from memory into the register until it reaches the low–order byte of the word in memory. The low–order (right–most) byte(s) of the register will not be changed.

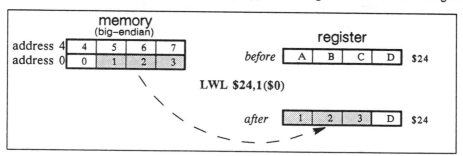

Load Word Left (continued)

LWL

The contents of general register *rt* are internally bypassed within the processor so that no NOP is needed between an immediately preceding load instruction which specifies register *rt* and a following LWL (or LWR) instruction which also specifies register *rt*.

Address error exceptions due to byte alignment are suppressed by this instruction.

Operation:

$$T: \quad vAddress \leftarrow (offset_{15})^{16} \parallel offset_{15..0} + GPR[base]$$
$$(pAddress, nonCacheable) \leftarrow AddrTranslation (vAddress)$$
$$byte \leftarrow vAddress_{1..0}$$

if BigEndian then
$$\quad mem \leftarrow LoadMemory (nonCacheable, WORD-byte, pAddress)$$
else
$$\quad mem \leftarrow LoadMemory (nonCacheable, byte, pAddress_{31..2} \parallel 0^2)$$
endif

$$T + 1: \text{ if BigEndian then}$$
$$\quad GPR[rt] \leftarrow mem_{31-8^*byte..0} \parallel GPR[rt]_{8^*byte-1..0}$$
else
$$\quad GPR[rt] \leftarrow mem_{7+8^*byte..0} \parallel GPR[rt]_{23-8^*byte..0}$$
endif

Exceptions:

UTLB miss fault
TLB miss fault
Bus error exception
Address error exception

LWR

Load Word Right

31	26	25	21	20	16	15	0
LWR		base		rt		offset	
6		5		5		16	

Format:

LWR rt,offset(base)

Description:

This instruction can be used in combination with the LWL instruction to load a register with four consecutive bytes from memory, when the bytes cross a boundary between two words. LWR loads the right portion of the register from the appropriate part of the low–order word; LWL loads the left portion of the register from the appropriate part of the high–order word.

The LWR instruction adds its sign–extended 16–bit *offset* to the contents of general register *base* to form a 32–bit unsigned effective address which can specify an arbitrary byte. It reads bytes **only** from the word in memory which contains the specified starting byte. From one to four bytes will be loaded, depending on the starting byte specified.

Conceptually, it starts at the specified byte in memory and loads that byte into the low–order (right–most) byte of the register; then it proceeds toward the high–order byte of the word in memory and the high–order byte of the register, loading bytes from memory into the register until it reaches the high–order byte of the word in memory. The high–order (left–most) byte(s) of the register will not be changed.

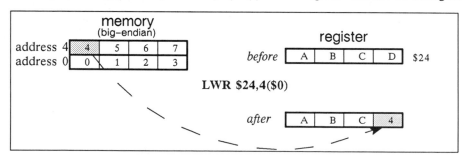

Load Word Right (continued)

LWR

The contents of general register *rt* are internally bypassed within the processor so that no NOP is needed between an immediately preceding load instruction which specifies register *rt* and a following LWR (or LWL) instruction which also specifies register *rt*.

Address error exceptions due to byte alignment are suppressed by this instruction.

Operation:

T: $vAddress \leftarrow (offset_{15})^{16} \parallel offset_{15..0} + GPR[base]$
$(pAddress, nonCacheable) \leftarrow AddrTranslation (vAddress)$
$byte \leftarrow vAddress_{1..0}$
if BigEndian then
    $mem \leftarrow LoadMemory (nonCacheable, byte, pAddress_{31..2} \parallel 0^2)$
else
    $mem \leftarrow LoadMemory (nonCacheable, byte, WORD-byte, pAddress)$
endIf

T + 1: if BigEndian then
    $GPR[rt] \leftarrow GPR[rt]_{31..8+8*byte} \parallel mem_{31..24-8*byte}$
else
    $GPR[rt] \leftarrow GPR[rt]_{31..24-8*byte} \parallel mem_{31..8+8*byte}$
endif

Exceptions:

UTLB miss fault
TLB miss fault
Bus error exception
Address error exception

MFC0

**Move From
System Control Coprocessor**

COP0	MF	rt	rd	0
6	5	5	5	11

Bit positions: 31 · 26 25 · 21 20 · 16 15 · 11 10 · 0

Format:

MFC0   rt,rd

Description:

The contents of coprocessor register rd of System Control Coprocessor (CP0) are loaded into general register rt.

Operation:

$$
\begin{array}{ll}
T: & \text{data} \leftarrow CPR[0, rd] \\
T + 1: & GPR[rt] \leftarrow \text{data}
\end{array}
$$

Exceptions:

Coprocessor unusable exception

Move From Coprocessor

MFCz

31	26	25	21	20	16	15	11	10	0
COPz		MF		rt		rd		0	
6		5		5		5		11	

Format:

MFCz   rt,rd

Description:

The contents of coprocessor register *rd* of coprocessor unit z are loaded into general register *rt*.

Operation:

```
T:    data ← CPR[z,rd]
T+1:  GPR[rt] ← data
```

Exceptions:

Coprocessor unusable exception

MFHI

Move From HI

31	26 25	16 15	11 10	6 5	0
SPECIAL	0	rd	0	MFHI	
6	10	5	5	6	

Format:

MFHI   rd

Description:

The contents of special register HI are loaded into general register *rd*.

To ensure proper operation in the event of interruptions, the two instructions which follow a MFHI instruction may not be any of the instructions which modify the HI register: MULT, MULTU, DIV, DIVU, MTHI.

Operation:

T:	GPR[rd]← HI

Exceptions:

None.

Move From Lo   **MFLO**

31 26	25 16	15 11	10 6	5 0
SPECIAL	0	rd	0	MFLO
6	10	5	5	6

Format:

MFLO rd

Description:

The contents of special register LO are loaded into general register *rd*.

To ensure proper operation in the event of interruptions, the two instructions which follow a MFLO instruction may not be any of the instructions which modify the LO register: MULT, MULTU, DIV, DIVU, MTLO.

Operation:

T:	GPR[rd] ← LO

Exceptions:

None.

MTC0

Move To
System Control Coprocessor

31 26	25 21	20 16	15 11	10 0
COP0	MT	rt	rd	0
6	5	5	5	11

Format:

MTC0 rt,rd

Description:

The contents of general register *rt* are loaded into coprocessor register *rd* of the System Control Coprocessor (CP0).

Because the state of the virtual address translation system may be altered by this instruction, the operation of load and store instructions and TLB operations immediately prior to and after this instruction are undefined.

Operation:

```
T:      data ←GPR[rt]
T + 1:  CPR[0,rd] ←data
```

Exceptions:

Coprocessor unusable exception

Move To Coprocessor

MTCz

31 26	25 21	20 16	15 11	10 0
COPz	MT	rt	rd	0
6	5	5	5	11

Format:

MTCz   rt,rd

Description:

The contents of general register *rt* are loaded into coprocessor register *rd* of coprocessor unit *z*.

Operation:

```
T:    data← GPR[rt]
T+1:  CPR[z,rd] ← data
```

Exceptions:

Coprocessor unusable exception

MTHI

Move To HI

SPECIAL	rs	0	MTHI

31 26 25	21 20	6 5	0
6	5	15	6

Format:

MTHI   rs

Description:

The contents of general register *rs* are loaded into special register HI.

If a MTHI operation is executed following a MULT, MULTU, DIV, or DIVU instruction, but before any MFLO, MFHI, MTLO, or MTHI instructions, the contents of special register LO are undefined.

Operation:

```
T-2:      HI  ← undefined

T-1:      HI  ← undefined

 T:       HI  ← GPR[rs]
```

Exceptions:

None.

Move To LO   # MTLO

31 26	25 21	20 6	5 0
SPECIAL	rs	0	MTLO
6	5	15	6

Format:

MTLO rs

Description:

The contents of general register *rs* are loaded into special register LO.

If a MTLO operation is executed following a MULT, MULTU, DIV, or DIVU instruction, but before any MFLO, MFHI, MTLO, or MTHI instructions, the contents of special register HI are undefined.

Operation:

```
T-2:      LO ← undefined
T-1:      LO ← undefined
T:        LO ← GPR[rs]
```

Exceptions:

None.

MULT
Multiply

31 26	25 21	20 16	15 6	5 0
SPECIAL	rs	rt	0	MULT
6	5	5	10	6

Format:

MULT rs,rt

Description:

The contents of general register *rs* and the contents of general register *rt* are multiplied, treating both operands as 32–bit two's complement values. No overflow exception occurs under any circumstances.

When the operation completes, the low–order word of the double result is loaded into special register LO, and the high–order word of the double result is loaded into special register HI. The MFHI and MFLO instructions are interlocked so that any attempt to read them before operations have completed will cause execution of instructions to be delayed until the operation finishes.

Multiply operations are performed by a separate, autonomous execution unit within the R2000. After a multiply operation is started, execution of other instructions may continue in parallel. The multiply/divide unit continues to operate during cache miss and other delaying cycles in which no instructions are executed.

Operation:

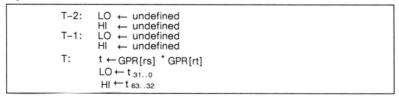

```
T-2:    LO ← undefined
        HI ← undefined
T-1:    LO ← undefined
        HI ← undefined
T:      t ← GPR[rs] * GPR[rt]
        LO ← t 31..0
        HI ← t 63..32
```

Exceptions:

None.

Multiply Unsigned

MULTU

31 26	25 21	20 16	15 6	5 0
SPECIAL	rs	rt	0	MULTU
6	5	5	10	6

Format:

MULTU rs,rt

Description:

The contents of general register *rs* and the contents of general register *rt* are multiplied, treating both operands as 32-bit unsigned values. No overflow exception occurs under any circumstances.

When the operation completes, the low-order word of the double result is loaded into special register LO, and the high-order word of the double result is loaded into special register HI. The MFHI and MFLO instructions are interlocked so that any attempt to read them before operations have completed will cause execution of instructions to be delayed until the operation finishes.

Multiply operations are performed by a separate, autonomous execution unit within the R2000. After a multiply operation is started, execution of other instructions may continue in parallel. The multiply/divide unit continues to operate during cache miss and other delaying cycles in which no instructions are executed.

Operation:

$$
\begin{aligned}
\text{T-2:} \quad & \text{LO} \leftarrow \text{undefined} \\
& \text{HI} \leftarrow \text{undefined} \\
\text{T-1:} \quad & \text{LO} \leftarrow \text{undefined} \\
& \text{HI} \leftarrow \text{undefined} \\
\text{T:} \quad & t \leftarrow (0 \parallel \text{GPR[rs]}) * (0 \parallel \text{GPR[rt]}) \\
& \text{LO} \leftarrow t_{31..0} \\
& \text{HI} \leftarrow t_{63..32}
\end{aligned}
$$

Exceptions:

None.

NOR

Nor

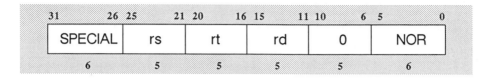

Format:

NOR   rd,rs,rt

Description:

The contents of general register *rs* are combined with the contents of general register *rt* in a bit–wise logical NOR operation. The result is placed into general register *rd*.

Operation:

T:	GPR[rd] ← GPR[rs] *nor* GPR[rt]

Exceptions:

None.

Or   OR

31 26	25 21	20 16	15 11	10 6	5 0
SPECIAL	rs	rt	rd	0	OR
6	5	5	5	5	6

Format:

OR   rd,rs,rt

Description:

The contents of general register *rs* are combined with the contents of general register *rt* in a bit–wise logical OR operation. The result is placed into general register *rd*.

Operation:

> |:   GPR[rd] ← GPR[rs] or GPR[rt]

Exceptions:

None.

ORI   Or Immediate

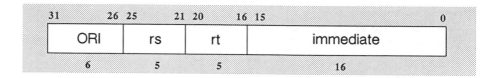

Format:

ORI rt,rs,immediate

Description:

The 16-bit *immediate* is zero-extended and combined with the contents of general
register *rs* in a bit-wise logical OR operation. The result is placed into general
register *rt*.

Operation:

T:	$GPR[rt] \leftarrow GPR[rs]_{31...16} \parallel (immediate \; or \; GPR[rs]_{15..0})$

Exceptions:

None.

Restore From Exception — RFE

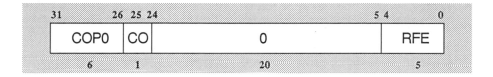

31	26	25	24		5	4	0
COP0		CO		0		RFE	
6		1		20		5	

Format:

RFE

Description:

Restores the *previous* interrupt mask and kernel/user–mode bits (IEp and KUp) of the Status register (SR) into the corresponding *current* status bits (IEc and KUc), and restores the *old* status bits (IEo and KUo) into the corresponding status bits (IEp and KUp). The *old* status bits remain unchanged.

The operation of memory references associated with load/store instructions immediately prior to an RFE instruction are unspecified. Normally, the RFE instruction follows in the delay slot of a JR (jump register) instruction to restore the PC.

Operation:

$$T: \quad SR \leftarrow SR_{31..4} \parallel SR_{5..2}$$

Exceptions:

Coprocessor unusable exception

SB

Store Byte

31 26	25 21	20 16	15 0
SB	base	rt	offset
6	5	5	16

Format:

SB rt,offset(base)

Description:

The 16–bit *offset* is sign–extended and added to the contents of general register *base* to form a 32–bit unsigned effective address. The least significant byte of the contents of register *rt* is stored at the effective address.

Operation:

```
T:       vAddress← (offset 15) 16 ‖ offset 15..0  +GPR[base]
         (pAddress, nonCacheable) ← AddrTranslation (vAddress)
         byte ← vAddress 1..0

         if BigEndian then
              data ←GPR[rt] 7+8*byte..0 ‖ 0 24..8*byte
         else
              data ←GPR[rt] 31-8*byte..0 ‖ 0 8*byte
         endif

T +1:    StoreMemory (nonCacheable, BYTE, data, pAddress)
```

Exceptions:

UTLB miss fault
TLB miss fault
TLB modification fault
Bus error exception
Address error exception

Store Halfword

SH

31 26	25 21	20 16	15 0
SH	base	rt	offset
6	5	5	16

Format:

SH   rt,offset(base)

Description:

The 16-bit *offset* is sign-extended and added to the contents of general register *base* to form a 32-bit unsigned effective address. The least significant halfword of the contents of register *rt* is stored at the effective address.

If the least significant bit of the effective address is non-zero, an address error exception occurs.

Operation:

```
T:      vAddress ← (offset 15) 16 ∥ offset 15..0  +GPR[base]
        (pAddress, nonCacheable) ← AddrTranslation (vAddress)
        byte ← vAddress 1..0
        if BigEndian then
              data ← GPR[rt] 15 +8*byte..0 ∥ 0 15-8*byte
        else
              data ← GPR[rt] 31-8*byte..0 ∥ 0 8*byte
        endif

T +1:   StoreMemory (nonCacheable, HALFWORD. data,  pAddress)
```

Exceptions:

UTLB miss fault
TLB miss fault
TLB modification fault
Bus error exception
Address error exception

SLL

Shift Left Logical

31 26	25 21	20 16	15 11	10 6	5 0
SPECIAL	0	rt	rd	shamt	SLL
6	5	5	5	5	6

Format:

SLL rd,rt,shamt

Description:

The contents of general register *rt* are shifted left by *shamt* bits, inserting zeroes into the low order bits. The 32–bit result is placed in register *rd*.

Operation:

T: $GPR[rd] \leftarrow GPR[rt]_{31-shamt,.0} \parallel 0^{shamt}$

Exceptions:

None.

Shift Left Logical Variable

SLLV

31 26	25 21	20 16	15 11	10 6	5 0
SPECIAL	rs	rt	rd	0	SLLV
6	5	5	5	5	6

Format:

SLLV rd,rt,rs

Description:

The contents of general register *rt* are shifted left by the number of bits specified by the low-order 5 bits of the contents of general register *rs*, inserting zeroes into the low order bits. The 32-bit result is placed in register *rd*.

Operation:

$$T: \qquad GPR[rd] \leftarrow GPR[rt]_{(31-GPR[rs]_{4..0})..0} \parallel 0^{GPR[rs]_{4..0}}$$

Exceptions:

None.

SLT

Set On Less Than

31	26	25	21	20	16	15	11	10	6	5	0
SPECIAL		rs		rt		rd		0		SLT	
6		5		5		5		5		6	

Format:

SLT rd,rs,rt

Description:

The contents of general register *rt* are compared with the contents of general register *rs*. Considering both quantities as signed 32–bit integers, if the contents of general register *rs* are less than the contents of general register *rt*, the result is set to one, otherwise the result is set to zero. The result is placed into general register *rd*.

No overflow exception occurs under any circumstances. The comparison is valid even if the subtraction used during the comparison overflows.

Operation:

T: if GPR[rs]< GPR[rt] then
            GPR[rd] ← 0^{31} ‖ 1
        else
            GPR[rd] ← 0^{32}
        endif

Exceptions:

None.

Set On Less Than Immediate   SLTI

31   26 25   21 20   16 15   0
SLTI	rs	rt	immediate
6	5	5	16

Format:

SLTI rt,rs,immediate

Description:

The 16-bit *immediate* is sign-extended and compared with the contents of general register *rs*. Considering both quantities as signed 32-bit integers, if *rs* is less than the sign-extended immediate, the result is set to one, otherwise the result is set to zero. The result is placed into general register *rt*.

No overflow exception occurs under any circumstances. The comparison is valid even if the subtraction used during the comparison overflows.

Operation:

$$
\begin{aligned}
T: \quad & \text{if } GPR[rs] < ((immediate_{15})^{16} \parallel immediate_{15..0}) \text{ then} \\
& \quad GPR[rt] \leftarrow 0^{31} \parallel 1 \\
& \text{else} \\
& \quad GPR[rt] \leftarrow 0^{32} \\
& \text{endif}
\end{aligned}
$$

Exceptions:

None.

Set On Less Than Immediate Unsigned

SLTIU

31 26	25 21	20 16	15 0
SLTIU	rs	rt	immediate
6	5	5	16

Format:

SLTIU rt,rs,immediate

Description:

The 16–bit *immediate* is sign–extended and compared with the contents of general register *rs*. Considering both quantities as unsigned 32–bit integers, if *rs* is less than the sign–extended immediate, the result is set to one, otherwise the result is set to zero. The result is placed into general register *rt*.

No overflow exception occurs under any circumstances. The comparison is valid even if the subtraction used during the comparison overflows.

Operation:

T: if $(0 \parallel GPR[rs]) < (0 \parallel immediate_{15})^{16} \parallel immediate_{15..0})$ then
        $GPR[rt] \leftarrow 0^{31} \parallel 1$
     else
        $GPR[rt] \leftarrow 0^{32}$
     endif

Exceptions:

None.

SLTU

Set On Less Than Unsigned

31 26	25 21	20 16	15 11	10 6	5 0
SPECIAL	rs	rt	rd	0	SLTU
6	5	5	5	5	6

Format:

SLTU   rd,rs,rt

Description:

The contents of general register *rt* are compared with the contents of general register *rs*. Considering both quantities as unsigned 32–bit integers, if the contents of general register *rs* are less than the contents of general register *rt*, the result is set to one, otherwise the result is set to zero. The result is placed into general register *rd*.

No overflow exception occurs under any circumstances. The comparison is valid even if the subtraction used during the comparison overflows.

Operation:

```
T:       if (0 ‖ GPR[rs])  <  (0 ‖ GPR[rt]) then
             GPR[rd] ← 0^31 ‖ 1
         else
             GPR[rd] ← 0^32
         endif
```

Exceptions:

None.

SRA

Shift Right Arithmetic

31 26	25 21	20 16	15 11	10 6	5 0
SPECIAL	0	rt	rd	shamt	SRA
6	5	5	5	5	6

Format:

SRA rd,rt,shamt

Description:

The contents of general register *rt* are shifted right by *shamt* bits, sign-extending the high order bits. The 32-bit result is placed in register *rd*.

Operation:

$$T: \quad GPR[rd] \leftarrow (GPR[rt]_{31})^{shamt} \parallel GPR[rt]_{31..shamt}$$

Exceptions:

None.

Shift Right Arithmetic Variable

SRAV

31 26	25 21	20 16	15 11	10 6	5 0
SPECIAL	rs	rt	rd	0	SRAV
6	5	5	5	5	6

Format:

SRAV rd,rt,rs

Description:

The contents of general register *rt* are shifted right by the number of bits specified by the low-order 5 bits of the contents of general register *rs*, sign-extending the high order bits. The 32-bit result is placed in register *rd*.

Operation:

$$\text{T:} \quad \text{GPR}[rd] \leftarrow (\text{GPR}[rt]_{31})^{\text{GPR}[rs]_{4..0}} \| \text{GPR}[rt]_{31..(\text{GPR}[rs]_{4..0})}$$

Exceptions:

None.

SRL

Shift Right Logical

31 26	25 21	20 16	15 11	10 6	5 0
SPECIAL	0	rt	rd	shamt	SRL
6	5	5	5	5	6

Format:

SRL rd,rt,shamt

Description:

The contents of general register *rt* are shifted right by *shamt* bits, inserting zeroes into the high order bits. The 32–bit result is placed in register *rd*.

Operation:

T: $GPR[rd] \leftarrow 0^{shamt} \parallel GPR[rt]_{31..shamt}$

Exceptions:

None.

Shift Right Logical Variable — **SRLV**

31 26	25 21	20 16	15 11	10 6	5 0
SPECIAL	rs	rt	rd	0	SRLV
6	5	5	5	5	6

Format:

SRLV rd,rt,rs

Description:

The contents of general register *rt* are shifted right by the number of bits specified by the low–order 5 bits of the contents of general register *rs,* inserting zeroes into the high order bits. The 32–bit result is placed in register *rd*.

Operation:

$$T: \quad GPR[rd] \leftarrow 0^{GPR[rs]_4..0} \| GPR[rt]_{31..(GPR[rs]_{4..0})}$$

Exceptions:

None.

SUB

Subtract

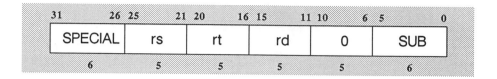

Format:

SUB rd,rs,rt

Description:

The contents of general register *rt* are subtracted from the contents of general register *rs* to form a 32–bit result. The result is placed into general register *rd*.

An overflow exception occurs if the two highest order carry–out bits differ (two's complement overflow).

Operation:

```
T:          GPR[rd] ←GPR[rs] – GPR[rt]
```

Exceptions:

Overflow exception

Subtract Unsigned   **SUBU**

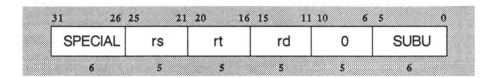

Format:

SUBU rd,rs,rt

Description:

The contents of general register *rt* are subtracted from the contents of general register *rs* to form a 32–bit result. The result is placed into general register *rd*.

No overflow exception occurs under any circumstances.

Note that the only difference between this instruction and the SUB instruction is that SUBU never causes an overflow exception.

Operation:

T:	GPR[rd] ←GPR[rs] − GPR[rt]

Exceptions:

None.

SW

Store Word

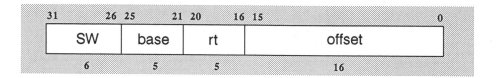

31 26	25 21	20 16	15 0
SW	base	rt	offset
6	5	5	16

Format:

SW rt,offset(base)

Description:

The 16-bit *offset* is sign-extended and added to the contents of general register *base* to form a 32-bit unsigned effective address. The contents of general register *rt* are stored at the memory location specified by the effective address.

If either of the two least significant bits of the effective address is non-zero, an address error exception occurs.

Operation:

$$
\begin{aligned}
\text{T:} \quad & \text{vAddress} \leftarrow (\text{offset}_{15})^{16} \,\|\, \text{offset}_{15..0} + \text{GPR[base]} \\
& (\text{pAddress, nonCacheable}) \leftarrow \text{AddrTranslation (vAddress)} \\
& \text{data} \leftarrow \text{GPR[rt]} \\
\text{T +1:} \quad & \text{StoreMemory (nonCacheable, WORD, data, pAddress)}
\end{aligned}
$$

Exceptions:

UTLB miss fault
TLB miss fault
TLB modification fault
Bus error exception
Address error exception

Store Word From Coprocessor

SWCz

SWCz	base	rt	offset
31 26	25 21	20 16	15 0
6	5	5	16

Format:

SWCz   rt,offset(base)

Description:

The 16-bit *offset* is sign-extended and added to the contents of general register *base* to form a 32-bit unsigned effective address. The contents of coprocessor register *rt* of coprocessor unit z are stored at the memory location specified by the effective address.

If either of the two least significant bits of the effective address is non-zero, an address error exception occurs.

Operation:

$$
\begin{aligned}
&T: \quad vAddress \leftarrow (offset_{15})^{16} \parallel offset_{15..0}) + GPR[base] \\
&\qquad (pAddress, nonCacheable) \leftarrow AddrTranslation (vAddress) \\
&\qquad data \leftarrow CPR[z,t] \\
&T+1: \quad StoreMemory (nonCacheable, 15, data, pAddress_{01..2} \parallel 0^2)
\end{aligned}
$$

Exceptions:

UTLB miss fault
TLB miss fault
TLB modification fault
Bus error exception
Address error exception
Coprocessor unusable exception

SWL

Store Word Left

31 26	25 21	20 16	15 0
SWL	base	rt	offset
6	5	5	16

Format:

SWL rt,offset(base)

Description:

This instruction can be used with the SWR instruction to store the contents of a register into four consecutive bytes of memory, when the bytes cross a boundary between two words. SWL stores the left portion of the register into the appropriate part of the high–order word of memory; SWR stores the right portion of the register into the appropriate part of the low–order word.

The SWL instruction adds its sign–extended 16–bit *offset* to the contents of general register *base* to form a 32–bit unsigned effective address which may specify an arbitrary byte. It alters **only** the word in memory which contains that byte. From one to four bytes will be stored, depending on the starting byte specified.

Conceptually, it starts at the high–order byte of the register and copies it to the specified byte in memory; then it proceeds toward the low–order byte of the register and the low–order byte of the word in memory, copying bytes from register to memory until it reaches the low–order byte of the word in memory.

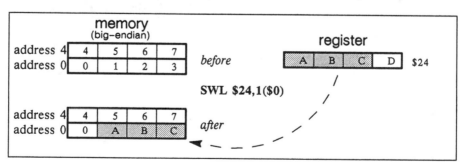

Store Word Left (continued)

SWL

Address error exceptions due to byte alignment are suppressed by this instruction.

Operation:

T: $vAddress \leftarrow (offset_{15})^{16} \parallel offset_{15..0} + GPR[base]$
        $(pAddress, nonCacheable) \leftarrow AddrTranslation (vAddress)$
        $byte \leftarrow vAddress_{1..0}$

        if BigEndian then
            $data \leftarrow 0^{8*byte} \parallel GPR[rt]_{31..8*byte}$
        else
            $data \leftarrow 0^{24-8*byte} \parallel GPR[rt]_{31..24-8*byte}$
        endif

T + 1: if BigEndian then
            StoreMemory (nonCacheable, WORD–byte, data, pAddress)
        else
            StoreMemory (nonCacheable, byte, data, $pAddress_{31..2} \parallel 0^2$)
        endif

Exceptions:

UTLB miss fault
TLB miss fault
TLB modification fault
Bus error exception
Address error exception

SWR   Store Word Right

31	26 25	21 20	16 15 0
SWR	base	rt	offset
6	5	5	16

Format:

SWR rt,offset(base)

Description:

This instruction can be used with the SWL instruction to store the contents of a register into four consecutive bytes of memory, when the bytes cross a boundary between two words. SWR stores the right portion of the register into the appropriate part of the low–order word; SWL stores the left portion of the register into the appropriate part of the low–order word of memory.

The SWR instruction adds its sign–extended 16–bit *offset* to the contents of general register *base* to form a 32–bit unsigned effective address which may specify an arbitrary byte. It alters **only** the word in memory which contains that byte. From one to four bytes will be stored, depending on the starting byte specified.

Conceptually, it starts at the low–order (right–most) byte of the register and copies it to the specified byte in memory; then it proceeds toward the high–order byte of the register and the high–order byte of the word in memory, copying bytes from register to memory until it reaches the high–order byte of the word in memory.

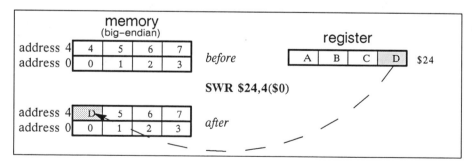

R2000 Architecture

Store Word Right (continued) {SWR}

SWR

Address error exceptions due to byte alignment are suppressed by this instruction.

Operation:

T: $vAddress \leftarrow (offset_{15})^{16} \| offset_{15..0} + GPR[base]$
      $(pAddress, nonCacheable) \leftarrow AddrTranslation (vAddress)$
      $byte \leftarrow vAddress_{1..0}$
      If BigEndian then
          $data \leftarrow GPR[rt]_{7+8*byte..0} \| 0^{24-8*byte}$
      else
          $data \leftarrow GPR[rt]_{31-8*byte..0} \| 0^{8*byte}$
      endif

T +1: if BigEndian then
          $StoreMemory(nonCacheable, byte, data, pAddress_{31..2} \| 0^2)$
      else
          $StoreMemory (nonCacheable, WORD-byte, data, pAddress)$
      endif

Exceptions:

UTLB miss fault
TLB miss fault
TLB modification fault
Bus error exception
Address error exception

SYSCALL

System Call

31 26	25 6	5 0
SPECIAL	0	SYSCALL
6		6

Format:

SYSCALL

Description:

A system call trap occurs, immediately and unconditionally transferring control to the exception handler.

Operation:

PC ← ExceptionHandler

Exceptions:

System Call trap

Probe TLB For Matching Entry

TLBP

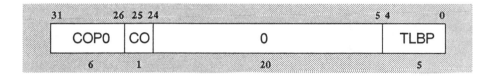

31		26	25	24		5	4		0
COP0			CO		0			TLBP	
6			1		20			5	

Format:

TLBP

Description:

The Index register is loaded with the address of the TLB entry whose contents match the contents of the EntryHi and EntryLo registers. If no TLB entry matches, the high-order bit of the Index register is set.

If more than one TLB entry matches, the results of this instruction are not specified. Additionally, the operation of memory references associated with the instruction immediately following a TLBP instruction is unspecified.

Operation:

```
T:      Index ←1 ‖ 0³¹
        for i in 0..TLBEntries-1
            if (TLB₆₃..₄₄[i] = EntryHi₃₁..₁₂) and
                (TLB₈ or (TLB₄₃..₃₈ = EntryHi₁₁..₆ ))) then
                    Index ← 0¹⁸ ‖ i₅..₀ ‖ 0⁸
            endif
        endfor
```

$$T: \quad Index \leftarrow 1 \parallel 0^{31}$$
$$\text{for } i \text{ in } 0..TLBEntries-1$$
$$\quad \text{if } (TLB_{63..44}[i] = EntryHi_{31..12}) \text{ and}$$
$$\quad\quad (TLB_8 \text{ or } (TLB_{43..38} = EntryHi_{11..6})) \text{) then}$$
$$\quad\quad\quad Index \leftarrow 0^{18} \parallel i_{5..0} \parallel 0^8$$
$$\quad \text{endif}$$
$$\text{endfor}$$

Exceptions:

Coprocessor unusable exception

TLBR

Read Indexed TLB Entry

31	26	25	24		5	4	0
COP0		CO		0		TLBR	
6		1		20		5	

Format:

TLBR

Description:

The EntryHi and EntryLo registers are loaded with the contents of the TLB entry pointed at by the contents of the TLB Index register.

The operation is invalid (and the results are unspecified) if the contents of the TLB Index register are greater than the number of TLB entries in the processor.

Operation:

$$T: \quad \text{EntryHi} \leftarrow \text{TLB}[\text{Index}_{13..8}]_{63..32}$$
$$\text{EntryLo} \leftarrow \text{TLB}[\text{Index}_{13..8}]_{31..0}$$

Exceptions:

Coprocessor unusable exception

Write Indexed TLB Entry

TLBWI

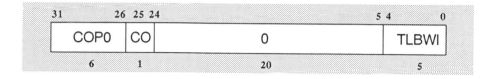

Format:

TLBWI

Description:

The TLB entry pointed at by the contents of the TLB Index register is loaded with the contents of the EntryHi and EntryLo registers.

The operation is invalid (and the results are unspecified) if the contents of the TLB Index register are greater than the number of TLB entries in the processor.

Operation:

$$T: \quad TLB[Index_{13..8}]_{63..32} \leftarrow EntryHi$$
$$TLB[Index_{13..8}]_{31..0} \leftarrow EntryLo$$

Exceptions:

Coprocessor unusable exception

TLBWR

Write Random TLB Entry

31	26	25	24		5	4	0
COP0		CO		0		TLBWR	
6		1		20		5	

Format:

TLBWR

Description:

The TLB entry pointed at by the contents of the TLB Random register is loaded with the contents of the EntryHi and EntryLo registers.

Operation:

$$T: \quad TLB[Random_{13..8}]_{63..32} \leftarrow EntryHi$$

$$TLB[Random_{13..8}]_{31..0} \leftarrow EntryLo$$

Exceptions:

Coprocessor unusable exception

Exclusive Or

XOR

31 26	25 21	20 16	15 11	10 6	5 0
SPECIAL	rs	rt	rd	0	XOR
6	5	5	5	5	6

Format:

XOR rd,rs,rt

Description:

The contents of general register *rs* are combined with the contents of general register *rt* in a bit–wise logical exclusive OR operation. The result is placed into general register *rd*.

Operation:

T:	GPR[rd] ← GPR[rs] *xor* GPR[rt]

Exceptions:

None.

XORI Exclusive Or Immediate

31 26	25 21	20 16	15 0
XORI	rs	rt	immediate
6	5	5	16

Format:

XORI rt,rs,immediate

Description:

The 16–bit *immediate* is zero–extended and combined with the contents of general register *rs* in a bit–wise logical exclusive–OR operation. The result is placed into general register *rt*.

Operation:

T: $GPR[rt] \leftarrow GPR[rs]_{31...16} \parallel (immediate \; xor \; GPR[rs]_{15..0})$

Exceptions:

None.

R2000 Instruction Opcode Bit Encoding

Opcode

31..29 \ 28..26	0	1	2	3	4	5	6	7
0	SPECIAL	BCOND	J	JAL	BEQ	BNE	BLEZ	BGTZ
1	ADDI	ADDIU	SLTI	SLTIU	ANDI	ORI	XORI	LUI
2	COP0	COP1	COP2	COP3	†	†	†	†
3	†	†	†	†	†	†	†	†
4	LB	LH	LWL	LW	LBU	LHU	LWR	†
5	SB	SH	SWL	SW	†	†	SWR	†
6	LWC0	LWC1	LWC2	LWC3	†	†	†	†
7	SWC0	SWC1	SWC2	SWC3	†	†	†	†

SPECIAL

5..3 \ 2..0	0	1	2	3	4	5	6	7
0	SLL	†	SRL	SRA	SLLV	†	SRLV	SRAV
1	JR	JALR	†	†	SYSCALL	BREAK	†	†
2	MFHI	MTHI	MFLO	MTLO	†	†	†	†
3	MULT	MULTU	DIV	DIVU	†	†	†	†
4	ADD	ADDU	SUB	SUBU	AND	OR	XOR	NOR
5	†	†	SLT	SLTU	†	†	†	†
6	†	†	†	†	†	†	†	†
7	†	†	†	†	†	†	†	†

BCOND

20..19 \ 18..16	0	1	2	3	4	5	6	7
0	BLTZ	BGEZ						
1								
2	BLTZAL	BGEZAL						
3								

COPz

22,21,16 \ 25..23	0	1	2	3	4	5	6	7
0,0,0	MF	MT	BCF					
0,0,1			BCT					
0,1,0								
0,1,1					CO			
1,0,0	CF	CT						
1,0,1								
1,1,0								
1,1,1								

COP0

4..3 \ 2..0	0	1	2	3	4	5	6	7
0		TLBR	TLBWI				TLBWR	
1	TLBP							
2	RFE							
3								

† Operation codes marked with a dagger cause reserved instruction exceptions and are reserved for future versions of the architecture.

This appendix provides a detailed description of the operation of each R2010 instruction. The instructions are listed alphabetically.

The exceptions that may occur due to the execution of each instruction are listed after the description of each instruction. The description of the immediate causes and manner of handling exceptions is omitted from the instruction descriptions in this chapter. Refer to **Chapter 8** for detailed descriptions of floating-point exceptions and handling.

Table B.4 at the end of this appendix lists the bit encoding for the constant fields of each instruction.

Instruction Formats

There are three basic instruction format types:

- I–Type, or Immediate instructions, which include Load and Store operations,
- M–Type, or Move instructions, and
- R–Type, or Register instructions, which include the two– and three–register Floating–Point operations.

The instruction description subsections that follow show how the three basic instruction formats are used by:

- Load and Store instructions,
- Move instructions, and
- Floating–Point Computational instructions.

A fourth instruction description subsection describes the special instruction format used by:

- Floating–Point Branch instructions.

Instruction Notational Conventions

In this appendix, all variable subfields in an instruction format (such as *fs, ft, immediate*, and so on) are shown with lower–case names. The instruction name (such as ADD, SUB, and so on) is shown in upper–case.

For the sake of clarity, an alias is sometimes substituted for a variable subfield in the formats of specific instructions. For example, we use *rs = base* in the format for Load and Store instructions. Such an alias is always lower case, since it refers to a variable subfield.

In some instructions, however, the two instruction subfields *op* and *function* have constant 6–bit values. When reference is made to these instructions, upper–case mnemonics are used. In the floating–point instruction, for example, we use *op* = COP1 and *function* = ADD. In some cases, a single field has both fixed and variable subfields, so the name contains both upper and lower case characters. Actual bit encoding for mnemonics is shown in Table B.5 at the end of this appendix.

In the instruction descriptions that follow, the *Operation* section describes the operation performed by each instruction using a high–level language notation. Special symbols used in the notation are described in Table B.1.

Table B.1 FPA Instruction Operation Notations

Symbol	Meaning
$\leftarrow$	Assignment
$\parallel$	Bit string concatenation
x^y	Replication of bit value x into a y-bit string. Note that x is always a single-bit value.
$x_{y..z}$	Selection of bits y through z of bit string x. Little-endian bit notation is always used. If y is less than z, this expression is an empty (zero length) bit string.
$+$	Two's complement or floating-point addition
$-$	Two's complement or floating-point subtraction
$*$	Two's complement or floating-point multiplication
div	Two's complement integer division
mod	Two's complement modulo
$<$	Two's complement less than comparison
and	Bitwise logic AND
or	Bitwise logic OR
xor	Bitwise logic XOR
nor	Bitwise logic NOR
GPR[x]	R2000 General Register x. Note that the contents of GPR[0] are always zero; attempts to alter GPR[0] contents have no effect.
FGR[x]	FPA General Register x. as viewed by the R2000 processor.
FPR[x]	FPA Floating-Point register x. Each FPR is assembled from two FGRs.
FCR[x]	FPA Control Register x
T+ i	Indicates the time steps (CPU cycles) between operations. Thus, operations identified as occurring at T+1 are performed during the cycle following the one where the instruction was initiated. This type of operation occurs with loads, stores, jumps, branches and coprocessor instructions.
virtualAddress	Virtual address
physicalAddress	Physical address

Instruction Notation Examples

The following examples illustrate the application of some of the instruction notation conventions:

Example #1:

$$\text{GPR[ft]} \leftarrow \text{immediate} \parallel 0^{16}$$

Sixteen zero bits are concatenated with an immediate value (typically 16 bits), and the 32-bit string (with the lower 16 bits set to zero) is assigned to GPR *ft.*

Example #2:

$$(\text{immediate}_{15})^{16} \parallel \text{immediate}_{15..0}$$

Bit 15 (the sign bit) of an immediate value is extended for 16 bit positions, and the result is concatenated with bits 15 through 0 of the immediate value to form a 32-bit sign-extended value.

Load and Store Instructions

All loads operations have a latency of one instruction. That is, the instruction immediately following a load cannot use the contents of the register which will be loaded with the data being fetched from storage.

In the load/store operation descriptions , the functions listed in Table B.2 are used to summarize the handling of virtual addresses and physical memory.

Function	Description
Addr Translation	Uses the TLB to find the physical address given the virtual address. The function fails and an exception is taken if the entry for the page containing the virtual address is not present in the TLB (Translation Lookaside Buffer).
Load Memory	Uses the cache and main memory to find the contents of the word containing the specified physical address. The low-order two bits of the address and the access type field indicate which of each of the four bytes within the data word need to be returned. If the cache is enabled for this access, the entire word is returned and loaded into the cache.
Store Memory	Uses the cache, write buffer, and main memory to store the word or part of word specified as data into the word containing the specified physical address. The low-order two bits of the address and the access type field indicate which of the four bytes within the data word should be stored.

Table B.2 Load/Store Common Functions

Load and Store Instruction Format

Figure B.1 shows the I–Type instruction format used by load and store operations.

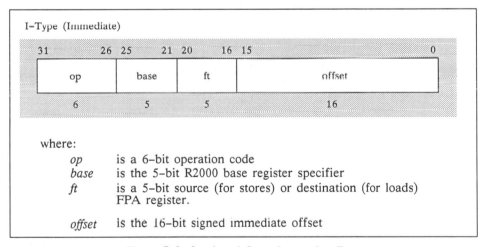

where:

  op   is a 6–bit operation code
  base   is the 5–bit R2000 base register specifier
  ft   is a 5–bit source (for stores) or destination (for loads) FPA register.

  offset is the 16–bit signed immediate offset

Figure B.1 Load and Store Instruction Format

All coprocessor loads and stores reference aligned full word data items. Thus, the access type field is always WORD, and the low-order two bits of the address must always be zero. The address specifies the smallest byte address of each byte in the address field.

Computational Instructions

Computational instructions include all of the arithmetic floating–point operations performed by the FPA.

Figure B.2 shows the R–Type instruction format used for computational operations.

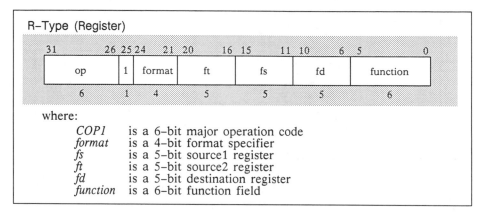

where:

COP1	is a 6–bit major operation code
format	is a 4–bit format specifier
fs	is a 5–bit source1 register
ft	is a 5–bit source2 register
fd	is a 5–bit destination register
function	is a 6–bit function field

Figure B.2 Computational Instruction Format

The four *format code* bits of a floating–point instruction specify which operand format is used in the instruction. Decoding for this field is shown in Table B.3.

Code	Mnemonic	Size	Format
0	S	single	binary floating–point
1	D	double	binary floating–point
2–3	–	–	reserved
4	W	single	binary fixed–point
5–15	–	–	reserved

Table B.3 Format Field Decoding

The six low–order *function* bits of coprocessor instruction indicate which floating–point operation is to be performed. Table B.4 lists all floating–point instructions.

Table B.4 Floating-Point Instructions and Operations

Code	Mnemonic	Operation
0	ADD.fmt	Add
1	SUB.fmt	Subtract
2	MUL.fmt	Multiply
3	DIV.fmt	Divide
4	–	reserved
5	ABS.fmt	Absolute value
6	MOV.fmt	Move
7	NEG.fmt	Negate
8–31	–	reserved
32	CVT.S.fmt	Convert to single floating-point
33	CVT.D.fmt	Convert to double floating-point
34–35	–	reserved
36	CVT.W.fmt	Convert to binary fixed-point
37–47	–	reserved
48–63	C.fmt	Floating-point compare

In the following pages, the notation *FGR* refers to the FPA's general registers 0 through 31, and *FPR* refers to the FPA's floating-point registers (FPR 0 through 30) which are formed by concatenation of FGR's (as described in **Chapter 6**).

The following routines are used in the description of the floating-point operations to get the value of an FPR or to change the value of an FGR. **NOTE:** When the format is single-precision or integer, the odd register of the destinations is undefined.

```
value ← ValueFPR(fp, fmt):
   case fmt of
      S: value ← FGR[fpr]
      D: value ← FGR[fpr + 1] ‖ FGR[fpr]
      W: value ← FGR[fpr]
   end
StoreFPR (fpr, fmt, value):
   case fmt of
      S: FGR[fpr + 1] ← undefined
         FGR[fpr]  ← value

      D: FGR[fpr + 1] ← value 63...32
         FGR[fpr]  ← value 31..0

      W: FGR[fpr] ← value
         FGR[fpr + 1] ← undefined
   end
```

ABS.fmt

Floating–Point Absolute Value

31 26	25	24 21	20 16	15 11	10 6	5 0
COP1	1	fmt	0	fs	fd	ABS
6	1	4	5	5	5	6

Format:

ABS.fmt   fd,fs

Description:

The contents of the FPA register specified by *fs* are interpreted in the specified format and the arithmetic absolute value is taken. The result is placed in the float-ing–point register specified by *fd*.

The absolute value is always exact.

On the FPA, this operation is valid only for single– and double–precision floating-point formats. This operation is not defined if bit 0 of any register specification is set, as the register numbers specify an even–odd pair of adjacent coprocessor gen-eral registers (FGR).

Operation:

```
T:     StoreFPR (fd, fmt, AbsoluteValue(ValueFPR (fs,fmt)));
```

Exceptions:

Coprocessor unusable exception
Coprocessor Exception Trap

Floating–Point Exceptions:

Unimplemented Operation Exception
Invalid Operation Exception

Floating–Point Add **ADD.fmt**

31	26	25	24	21	20	16	15	11	10	6	5	0
COP1		1	fmt		ft		fs		fd		ADD	
6		1	4		5		5		5		6	

Format:

ADD.fmt fd,fs,ft

Description:

The contents of the FPA registers specified by *fs* and *ft* are interpreted in the specified format and arithmetically added. The result is rounded as if calculated to infinite precision and then rounded to the specified format (*fmt*), according to the current rounding mode. The result is placed in the floating–point register (FPR) specified by *fd*.

This instruction is valid on the FPA only for single– and double–precision floating–point format. This operation is not defined if bit 0 of any register specification is set, as the register numbers specify an even–odd pair of adjacent FPA general registers (FGR).

Operation:

```
T:    StoreFPR (fd, fmt, ValueFPR(fs, fmt) + ValueFPR (ft, fmt));
```

Exceptions:

Coprocessor unusable exception
Coprocessor Exception Trap

Floating–Point Exceptions:

Unimplemented Operation Exception
Invalid Operation Exception
Inexact Exception
Overflow Exception
Underflow Exception

BC1F

**Branch On FPA False
(coprocessor 1)**

31 26	25 16	15 0
COP1	BCF	offset
6	10	16

Format:

BC1F   offset

Description:

A branch target address is computed from the sum of the address of the instruction in the delay slot and the 16-bit *offset*, shifted left two bits and sign-extended to 32 bits. If the FPA's condition signal (FpCond) to the R2000 Processor is false, the prgoram branches to the target address, with a delay of one instruction.

Operation:

```
T:      target ← (offset 15) 14 ‖ offset  ‖ 0²
        condition ← not CpCond[1]

T+1:    if condition  then
            PC ← PC + target
        endif
```

Exceptions:

Coprocessor unusable exception

Branch On FPA True (coprocessor 1)

BC1T

31 26	25 16	15 0
COP1	BCT	offset
6	10	16

Format:

BC1T   offset

Description:

A branch target address is computed from the sum of the address of the instruction in the delay slot and the 16-bit *offset*, shifted left two bits and sign-extended to 32 bits. If the FPA's condition signal (FpCond) to the R2000 Processor is true, the prgoram branches to the target address, with a delay of one instruction.

Operation:

$$
\begin{aligned}
\text{T:} \quad & \text{target} \leftarrow (\text{offset}_{15})^{14} \parallel \text{offset} \parallel 0^2 \\
& \text{condition} \leftarrow \text{CpCond}[1] \\
\text{I+1:} \quad & \text{if condition then} \\
& \quad \text{PC} \leftarrow \text{PC} + \text{target} \\
& \quad \text{endif}
\end{aligned}
$$

Exceptions:

Coprocessor unusable exception

C.cond.fmt

Floating–Point Compare

COP1	1	fmt	ft	fs	0	FC	cond
6	1	4	5	5	5	2	4

Bit positions: 31 — 26 25 24 — 21 20 — 16 15 — 11 10 — 6 5 4 3 — 0

Format:

C.cond.fmt   fs,ft

Description:

The contents of the FPA registers specified by *fs* and *ft* are interpreted in the specified source format and arithmetically compared. A result is determined based on
the comparison and the conditions specified in the instruction. If one of the values
is a NaN, and the low–order bit of the condition is set, an invalid operation trap is
taken. After a one–instruction delay, the condition is available for testing with
"branch on FPA coprocessor condition" instructions.

Comparisons are exact and neither overflow nor underflow. Four mutually exclusive relations are possible results: *less than, equal, greater than, and unordered*. The
last case arises when one or both of the operands are NaN; every NaN compares
unordered with everything, including itself. Comparisons ignore the sign of zero, so
+0 = −0.

On the FPA, this operation is valid only for double– or single–precision floating-
point formats. This operation is not defined if bit 0 of any register specification is
set, as the register numbers specify an even–odd pair of adjacent coprocessor general registers (FGR).

Floating-Point Compare (continued)

C.cond.fmt

Operation:

```
T:    if NaN(ValueFPR(fs, fmt))  or NaN(ValueFPR(ft, fmt)) then
          less  ←   false
          equal ←  false
          unordered ← true
          if cond₃  then
             signal InvalidOperationException
          endif
      else
          less ← ValueFPR(fs,rmt) < ValueFPR(ft,rmt)
          equal ← ValueFPR(fs,rmt) = ValueFPR(ft,rmt)
          unordered ← false
      endif
T+1:  condition ←   (cond₂ and less) or
          (cond₁ and equal) or
          (cond₀ and unordered)
```

Exceptions:

Coprocessor unusable exception
Coprocessor Exception Trap

Floating-Point Exceptions:

Unimplemented Operation Exception
Invalid Operation Exception

CFC1

**Move Control word from FPA
(coprocessor 1)**

31	26	25	21	20	16	15	11	10	0
COP1		CF		rt		fs		0	
6		5		5		5		11	

Format:

CFC1 rt,fs

Description:

The contents of the FPA's control register *fs* are loaded into R2000 Processor's general register *rt*.

Operation:

```
T:    temp  ←   FCR[fs];
T + 1:   GPR[rt] ← temp;
```

Exceptions:

Coprocessor unusable exception

Move Control word to FPA (coprocessor 1)

CTC1

COP1	CT	rt	fs	0
31 26	25 21	20 16	15 11	10 0
6	5	5	5	11

Format:

CTC1 rt,fs

Description:

The contents of R2000 Processor's general register *rt* arc loaded into the FPA's control (FCR) register *fs*.

Operation:

T: temp ← GPR[rt];

T + 1: FCR[fs] ← temp

Exceptions:

Coprocessor unusable exception

CVT.D.fmt

Floating–Point Convert to Double Floating–Point Format

31	26 25	24	21 20	16 15	11 10	6 5	0
COP1	1	fmt	0	fs	fd	CVT.D	
6	1	4	5	5	5	6	

Format:

CVT.D.fmt   fd,fs

Description:

The contents of the FPA register specified by *fs* are interpreted in the specified source format and arithmetically converted to the double binary floating–point format. The result is placed in the FPA register specified by *fd*.

Rounding occurs according to the currently specified rounding mode.

On the FPA, this operation is valid only for conversion from a single fixed–point or floating–point format. This operation is not defined if bit 0 of any register specification is set, as the register numbers specify an even–odd pair of adjacent coprocessor general registers (FGR).

Operation:

```
T:     StoreFPR (fd, D, ConvertFmt(ValueFPR(fs, fmt), fmt, D))
```

Exceptions:

Coprocessor unusable exception
Coprocessor Exception Trap

Floating–Point Exceptions:

Unimplemented Operation Exception
Invalid Operation Exception

Floating–Point Convert to Single Floating–Point Format

CVT.S.fmt

31 26	25 24	21 20	16 15	11 10	6 5	0
COP1	1	fmt	0	fs	fd	CVT.S
6	1	4	5	5	5	6

Format:

CVT.S.fmt fd,fs

Description:

The contents of the FPA register specified by *fs* are interpreted in the specified source format and arithmetically converted to the single binary floating–point format. The result is placed in the FPA register specified by *fd*.

Rounding occurs according to the currently specified rounding mode.

On the FPA, this operation is valid only for conversion from double–precision floating–point or fixed–point formats. This operation is not defined if bit 0 of any register specification is set, as the register numbers specify an even–odd pair of adjacent coprocessor general registers (FGR).

Operation:

```
T:     StoreFPR (fd, S, ConvertFmt(ValueFPR(fs, fmt), fmt, S))
```

Exceptions:

Coprocessor unusable exception
Coprocessor Exception Trap

Floating–Point Exceptions:

Unimplemented Operation Exception
Invalid Operation Exception

CVT.W.fmt

**Floating–Point Convert to
Fixed–Point Format**

31	26	25	24	21	20	16	15	11	10	6	5	0
COP1		1	fmt		0		fs		fd		CVT.W	
6		1	4		5		5		5		6	

Format:

CVT.W.fmt   fd,fs

Description:

The contents of the FPA register specified by *fs* are interpreted in the specified source format and arithmetically converted to the single fixed–point format. The result is placed in the FPA register specified by *fd*.

On the FPA, this operation is valid only for conversion from single– or double–precision floating–point formats. For double–precision format, this operation is not defined if bit 0 of any register specification is set, as the register numbers specify an even–odd pair of adjacent coprocessor general registers (FGR).

Operation:

T: StoreFPR (fd, W, ConvertFmt(ValueFPR(fs, fmt), fmt, W))

Exceptions:

Coprocessor unusable exception
Coprocessor Exception Trap

Floating–Point Exceptions:

Unimplemented Operation Exception
Invalid Operation Exception

Floating–Point Divide

DIV.fmt

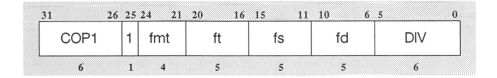

Format:

DIV.fmt   fd,fs,ft

Description:

The contents of the FPA registers specified by *fs* and *ft* are interpreted in the specified format and arithmetically divided. The result is rounded as if calculated to infinite precision and then rounded to the specified format (*fmt*), according to the current rounding mode. The result is placed in the floating–point register (FPR) specified by *fd*.

This instruction is valid on the FPA only for single– and double–precision floating–point format. This operation is not defined if bit 0 of any register specification is set, as the register numbers specify an even–odd pair of adjacent FPA general registers (FGR).

Operation:

```
T:     StoreFPR (fd, fmt, ValueFPR(fs, fmt)  / ValueFPR (ft, fmt));
```

Exceptions:

Coprocessor unusable exception
Coprocessor Exception Trap

Floating–Point Exceptions:

Unimplemented Operation Exception   Invalid Operation Exception
Inexact Exception   Overflow Exception
Divide by Zero Exception

LWC1

Load Word to FPA
(coprocessor 1)

31 26	25 21	20 16	15 0
LWC1	base	ft	offset
6	5	5	16

Format:

LWC1 ft,offset(base)

Description:

The 16–bit *offset* is sign–extended and added to the contents of the R2000 Processor's general register *base* to form a 32–bit unsigned effective address. The contents of the word at the effective address memory location is loaded into the FPA's general register (FGR) at location *ft*.

If either of the two least significant bits of the effective address is non–zero, an address error exception occurs.

Operation:

```
T:    virtualAddress ← (offset 15 ) 16 ‖ offset 15..0  + GPR[base];
      physicalAddress ← AddressTranslation (virtualAddress);
      mem← LoadMemory (WORD, physicalAddress);
      byte ← virtualAddress1..0 ;

T+1: FGR[ft]  ← mem
```

Exceptions:

Coprocessor unusable exception
Bus error exception
Address error exception

Move From FPA (coprocessor 1)

MFC1

31 26	25 21	20 16	15 11	10 0
COP1	MF	rt	fs	0
6	5	5	5	11

Format:

MFC1 rt,fs

Description:

The contents of the FPA general register at location *fs* are loaded into R2000 Processor's general register *rt*.

Operation:

```
T:    temp ← FGR[fs];
T+1:  GPR[rt] ← temp
```

Exceptions:

Coprocessor unusable exception

MOV.fmt   Floating–Point Move

31	26	25	24	21	20	16	15	11	10	6	5	0
COP1		1	fmt		0		fs		fd		MOV	
6		1	4		5		5		5		6	

Format:

MOV.fmt   fd,fs

Description:

The contents of the FPA register specified by *fs* are interpreted in the specified format and are copied into the FPA register specified by *fd*.

The Move operation is always exact.

On the FPA, this operation is valid only for single– and double–precision floating–point formats. This operation is not defined if bit 0 of any register specification is set, as the register numbers specify an even–odd pair of adjacent coprocessor general registers (FGR).

Operation:

```
T:      StoreFPR (fd, fmt, ValueFPR (fs, fmt));
```

Exceptions:

Coprocessor unusable exception
Coprocessor Exception Trap

Floating–Point Exceptions:

Unimplemented Operation Exception

Move To FPA (coprocessor 1)   MTC1

31	26	25	21	20	16	15	11	10	0
COP1		MT		rt		fs		0	
6		5		5		5		11	

Format:

MTC1 rt,fs

Description:

The contents of R2000 Processor's general register *rt* are loaded into the FPA's general register at location *fs*.

Operation:

```
T:    temp ← GPR[rt];
T+1:  FGR[fs]← data;
```

Exceptions:

Coprocessor unusable exception

MUL.fmt

Floating–Point Multiply

31	26	25 24	21 20	16 15	11 10	6 5	0
COP1	1	fmt	ft	fs	fd	MUL	
6	1	4	5	5	5	6	

Format:

MUL.fmt fd,fs,ft

Description:

The contents of the FPA registers specified by *fs* and *ft* are interpreted in the speci-fied format and arithmetically multiplied. The result is rounded as if calculated to infinite precision and then rounded to the specified format (*fmt*), according to the current rounding mode. The result is placed in the floating–point register (FPR) specified by *fd*.

This instruction is valid on the FPA only for single– and double–precision floating–point format. This operation is not defined if bit 0 of any register specification is set, as the register numbers specify an even–odd pair of adjacent FPA general regis-ters (FGR).

Operation:

```
T: StoreFPR (fd, fmt, ValueFPR(fs, fmt) * ValueFPR (ft, fmt));
```

Exceptions:

Coprocessor unusable exception
Coprocessor Exception Trap

Floating–Point Exceptions:

Unimplemented Operation Exception
Invalid Operation Exception
Inexact Exception
Overflow Exception
Underflow Exception

Floating-Point Negate

NEG.fmt

COP1	1	fmt	0	fs	fd	NEG
31 26	25 24	21 20	16 15	11 10	6 5	0
6	1	4	5	5	5	6

Format:

NEG.fmt fd,fs

Description:

The contents of the FPA register specified by *fs* are interpreted in the specified format and the arithmetic negation is taken (the polarity of the sign-bit is changed). The result is placed in the FPA register specified by *fd*. If the register contains a signaling NaN, an invalid Operation Exception is generated.

The negated value is always exact.

On the FPA, this operation is valid only for single- and double-precision floating-point formats. This operation is not defined if bit 0 of any register specification is set, as the register numbers specify an even-odd pair of adjacent coprocessor general registers (FGR).

Operation:

```
T:      StoreFPR (fd, fmt, Negate(ValueFPR(fs, fmt)))
```

Exceptions:

Coprocessor unusable exception
Coprocessor Exception Trap

Floating-Point Exceptions:

Unimplemented Operation Exception
Invalid Operation Exception

SUB.fmt

Floating–Point Subtract

31	26	25	24	21	20	16	15	11	10	6	5	0
COP1		1	fmt		ft		fs		fd		SUB	
6		1	4		5		5		5		6	

Format:

SUB.fmt fd,fs,ft

Description:

The contents of the FPA registers specified by *fs* and *ft* are interpreted in the speci-fied format and arithmetically subtracted. The result is rounded as if calculated to infinite precision and then rounded to the specified format (*fmt*), according to the current rounding mode. The result is placed in the floating–point register (FPR) specified by *fd*.

This instruction is valid on the FPA only for single– and double–precision floating-point format. This operation is not defined if bit 0 of any register specification is set, as the register numbers specify an even–odd pair of adjacent FPA general regis-ters (FGR).

Operation:

```
T:      StoreFPR (fd, fmt, ValueFPR(fs, fmt) – ValueFPR (ft, fmt));
```

Exceptions:

Coprocessor unusable exception
Coprocessor Exception Trap

Floating–Point Exceptions:

Unimplemented Operation Exception
Invalid Operation Exception
Inexact Exception
Overflow Exception
Underflow Exception

Store Word from FPA (coprocessor 1)

SWC1

31 26	25 21	20 16	15 0
SWC1	base	ft	offset
6	5	5	16

Format:

SWC1 ft,offset(base)

Description:

The 16-bit *offset* is sign-extended and added to the contents of the R2000 Processor's general register *base* to form a 32-bit unsigned effective address. The contents of the FPA's general register (FGR) at location *ft is* stored at the memory location specified by the effective address.

If either of the two least significant bits of the effective address is non-zero, an address error exception occurs.

Operation:

T: $virtualAddress \leftarrow (offset_{15})^{16} \parallel offset_{15..0} + GPR[base]$
        $physicalAddress \leftarrow AddressTranslation (virtualAddress);$
        $data \leftarrow FGR[ft]$

T+1: $StoreMemory (WORD, data, physicalAddress)$

Exceptions:

Coprocessor unusable exception
Bus error exception
Address error exception

R2010 FPA Instruction Opcode Bit Encoding

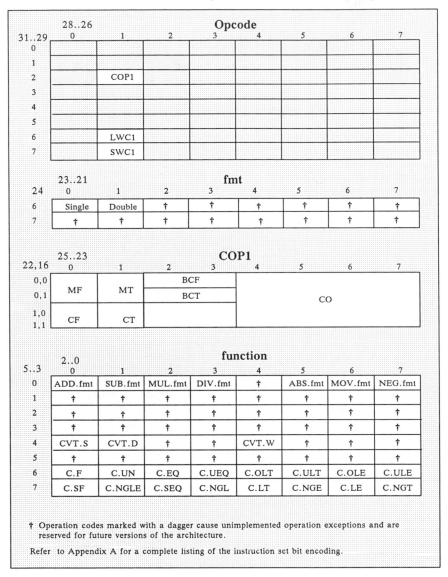

† Operation codes marked with a dagger cause unimplemented operation exceptions and are reserved for future versions of the architecture.

Refer to Appendix A for a complete listing of the instruction set bit encoding.

Table B.5 Bit Encoding for R2010 FPA Instructions

C
Machine Language Programming Tips

The RISC architecture implemented by the R2000 Processor provides an efficient, uniform, and streamlined instruction set to obtain maximum efficiency for the most commonly performed operations. As a result, some operations that would require single, multi-cycle instructions in more traditional architectures require multiple, single-cycle R2000 instructions.

The R2000 architecture also provides no condition code register containing status bits such as *Carry* and *Overflow*. Instead, the conditions generated by the Set instructions (**slt**, **sltu**) are loaded directly into a general-purpose register. This approach greatly simplifies handling of the instruction pipeline and eases many compiler tasks but does require that programs explicitly check for conditions such as overflow and carry.

This appendix describes techniques that can be used to implement the following operations:

- Handling 32-bit addresses or constants
- Implementing indexed addressing
- Using the Jump Register (**jr**) instruction for subroutine returns
- Jumping to 32-bit addresses
- Branching on arithmetic comparisons
- Filling the branch delay slot
- Testing for overflow
- Testing for carry
- Performing multi-precision math

Note that the MIPS assembly language supports many of these functions (such as loading 32-bit addresses and branching on arithmetic comparisons) that are not directly implemented by the R2000 machine language. It does this using techniques similar to those described in this appendix. Refer to **Appendix D** for an overview of the MIPS assembly language.

In many of the following examples, a temporary register is used to hold intermediate results. In the following description, **$at** is used to represent that temporary register, and it is assumed that the register is reserved for just this purpose and therefore doesn't conflict with anything else.

32–bit Addresses or Constants

The R2000 does not provide specific "load address" or "load immediate" instructions. (Note: the MIPS assembly language does provide load address (**la**) and load immediate (**li**) instructions that are implemented using multiple machine language instructions. To load an address with relocatable code, you *must* use the assembler's **la** instruction.) Use the following two–instruction sequence to load any 32–bit pattern into a register:

```
lui   $destination, <upper 16 bits>
ori   $destination, <lower 16 bits>
```

There are three special cases which require only one instruction to obtain the desired 32–bit pattern:

- **Constants with the upper 16 bits set to zero.** Use the **ori** instruction, which zero–extends the immediate field:

```
ori   $destination,$0,<lower 16 bits>
```

- **Constants with the upper 17 bits set to one.** Use the low–order 16 bits of the constant in the **addi** instruction, which sign–extends the immediate field:

```
addi $destination,$0,<lower 16 bits>
```

- **Constants with the lower 16 bits set to zero.** Use the high–order 16 bits of the constant in the **lui** instruction, which shifts its immediate field left by 16 bits, bringing in zeroes on the right:

```
lui $destination,<upper 16 bits>
```

Indexed Addressing

The R2000 provides only one addressing mode. This addressing mode sign–extends a 16–bit offset, adds it to the contents of a base register, and loads the destination (or stores the source) from (to) that memory address. The format for the load word (**lw**) instruction is shown below:

```
lw $destination,<16-bit offset>($baseregister)
```

(The following examples use the **lw** instruction to illustrate various addressing modes; the examples are, however, equally valid for other load and store instructions.)

More general addressing modes can be simulated by using additional instructions. For example, if the offset exceeds 16 bits, you can use **lui** and **addiu** to add the upper 16 bits to the base register, and you can put the lower 16 bits into the *offset* field of the **lw** instruction. Thus, you can implement:

```
lw $destination,<32-bit offset>($baseregister)
```

with:

```
lui  $at,<upper 16 bits adjusted>
addu $at,$at,$baseregister
lw   $destination,<lower 16 bits>($at)
```

Why the term *adjusted*? Because the **lw** instruction sign–extends the lower 16 bits, you must add 1 to the upper 16 bits if the lower 16 bits appears to be a negative number—if, in other words, a logical *AND* between the 32–bit constant and 0x8000 is non–zero. For example:

32–bit constant	upper 16 bits adjusted	lower 16 bits
0x04004000	0x0400	0x4000
0x04008000	0x0401	0x8000

The absence of a base register permits an even simpler instruction sequence, but still requires you to adjust the upper 16 bits. Thus, you can implement:

```
lw $destination,<32-bit address>
```

with:

```
lui  $at,<upper 16 bits adjusted>
lw   $destination,<lower 16 bits>($at)
```

Subroutine Return Using Jump Register Instruction

The subroutine call instructions, **jal** and **jalr**, put the return address into register $31. To return from a subroutine, use **jr $31**. If one subroutine needs to call yet another subroutine, the calling subroutine must save the value of $31 (on the stack, for example) before making the call, and restore the value of $31 upon return.

Jumping to 32–bit Addresses

The **j** and **jal** instructions, which contain an immediate field, can actually jump only within a 2^{28}–bit segment, because the instructions obtain the high–order four bits from the current program counter. To jump to an arbitrary 32–bit address, you must load the desired address into a temporary register (using the "load address" technique described earlier) and then use the jump register (**jr**) instruction:

```
la   $at,foo
jr $at
```

Branching On Arithmetic Comparisons

The R2000 provides a complete set of arithmetic comparisons against zero. (There are no instructions for **beqz** or **bnez**, but you can obtain the same effect by using register $0, which always contains a value of zero, in the **beq** and **bne** instructions). However, the only instructions for comparing a pair of registers are **beq** and **bne**. To perform any other arithmetic comparison on a pair of registers or between a register and an immediate value, you must use a sequence of two instructions as listed in Table C.1 or C.2.

Desired Instruction	Equivalent Sequence
beq $a,$b,dest	beq $a,$b,dest
bne $a,$b,dest	bne $a,$b,dest
blt $a,$b,dest	slt $at,$a,$b; bne $at,$0,dest
ble $a,$b,dest	slt $at,$b,$a; beq $at,$0,dest
bgt $a,$b,dest	slt $at,$b,$a; bne $at,$0,dest
bge $a,$b,dest	slt $at,$a,$b; beq $at,$0,dest
bltu $a,$b,dest	sltu $at,$a,$b; bne $at,$0,dest
bleq $a,$b,dest	sltu $at,$b,$a; beq $at,$0,dest
bgtu $a,$b,dest	sltu $at,$b,$a; bne $at,$0,dest
bgeu $a,$b,dest	sltu $at,$a,$b; beq $at,$0,dest

Table C.1 Arithmetic Comparisons on Register Pairs

Desired Instruction	Equivalent Sequence
beq $a,i,dest	li $at,i; beq $a,$at,dest
bne $a,i,dest	li $at,i; bne $a,$at,dest
blt $a,i,dest	slti $at,$a,i; bne $at,$0,dest
ble $a,i,dest	slti $at,$a,i+1; bne $at,$0,dest
bgt $a,i,dest	slti $at,$a,i+1; beq $at,$0,dest
bge $a,i,dest	slti $at,$a,i; beq $at,$0,dest

Table C.2 Arithmetic Comparisons with Immediate Values

Note that the MIPS assembly language supports all of the branch instructions listed in the Tables C.1 and C.2 by performing the equivalent two-instruction sequence. Refer to the *Assembly Language Programmer's Guide* for a description of these branch instructions.

Filling the Branch Delay Slot

You can sometimes save instructions by exploiting the knowledge that the instruction in the delay slot of a conditional branch will execute immediately after the comparison, regardless of whether the branch is taken. For example, compare a straightforward implementation of "$6 = maximum($5,$4)" with a tricky one. The straightforward implementation takes seven instructions if you count the "nop"s which the assembler will insert to fill the branch delay slots:

```
     slt $at,$5,$4
     beq $at,$0,1f  # if $5 >= $4 ...
     # nop (inserted by assembler to fill delay slot)
     addu $6,$4,$0  # else move $4 to $6
     b 2f
     # nop (inserted by assembler to fill delay slot)
1:   addu $6,$5,$0  # then move $5 to $6
2:
```

A tricky version takes only four instructions. Observe that it's harmless to use the delay slot to move one value into $6 while the conditional branch is being evaluated, and then--if the branch is not taken--override that by moving the other value into $6 instead. To put an instruction into the delay slot yourself, you must temporarily set the assembler to "no-reorder" mode, so that it will not fill the delay slot with a "nop" for you:

```
      .set noreorder
      slt $at,$5,$4
      beq $at,$0,1f  # if $5 >= $4 ...
      addu $6,$5,$0  # move $5 to $6 while evaluating "beq"
      addu $6,$4,$0  # if branch not taken, move $4 to $6 instead
1:
      .set reorder
```

To implement "minimum" instead of "maximum", just swap $5 and $4 in the "slt" instruction.

A similar trick works for "$6 = abs($5)":

```
      .set noreorder
      bgtz $5,1f     # if $5 > 0 ...
      addu $6,$5,$0  # move $5 to $6 while evaluating "bgt"
      subu $6,$0,$6  # if branch not taken, negate $6
1:
      .set reorder
```

Notice that the following sequence, which appears equivalent, is not entirely fool-proof, because it would fail if the destination register were the same as the source—such as "$5 = abs($5)":

```
     .set noreorder
     bltz $5,1f      # if $5 < 0
     subu $6,$0,$5   # negate $5 into $6 while evaluating "blt"
     addu $6,$5,$0   # if branch not taken, move $5 to $6 instead
                     # (but if $5 and $6 were the same, the
                     # register would already have been negated)
1:
     .set reorder
```

Testing for Carry

The R2000 does not provide a status bit to indicate whether an arithmetic operation resulted in a carry. Therefore, routines that require detection of a carry (or borrow) resulting from an addition (or subtraction) must explicitly test for their occurrence. This section provides examples of performing add–with–carry and subtract–with–borrow operations.

To perform an add–with–carry, a routine must first explicitly calculate whether the addition will result in a carry and record the occurrence of a carry in a register. When doing multi–word additions, a test is made to see if there is a carry in, and then two different code sequences are used to add the words: one sequence for adding with a carry in and one sequence for adding without a carry in. Both sequences can calculate the carry out.

For example, the following sequence calculates whether the addition of A and B with no carry in will result in a carry out:

```
# carryout from A + B
addu  temp,A,B
sltu  carryout,temp,B
```

If there is a carry in, the following sequence can be used to calculate whether the addition of A and B will result in a carry out:

```
# carryout from A + B + 1
not   temp,A
sltu  carryout,B,temp
xor   carryout,1
```

The technique for performing subtract–with–borrow is quite similar. Again, two sequences are used to calculate whether a subtraction will result in a borrow; one sequence for the case where there is no borrow in:

```
# borrow out from A - B
sltu  borrow,A,B
```

And a second routine for the case where there *is* a borrow in:

```
# borrow out from A - B - 1
sltu  borrow,B,A
xor   borrow,1
```

Testing for Overflow

The R2000 does not provide a status bit to indicate whether an arithmetic operation resulted in an overflow. The signed addition and subtraction instructions (**ADD** and **SUB**) trap if an overflow occurs and thus implement overflow detection at no cost. However, if it is necessary to detect signed overflow without using traps or to detect overflow for unsigned operations, the techniques described in this section can be used.

Figure C.1 provides examples of code that checks for overflow for various arithmetic operations. These examples are based on the following simple rules for signed overflow:

- During addition, overflow occurs if the signs of the addends are the same and the sign of the sum is different.

- During subtraction, overflow occurs if the signs of the operands are different and the sign of the resultant difference is not the same as the sign of the minuend.

Signed Addition

```
/* compute t0 = t1 + t2, branch to L on signed overflow */
      addu   t0, t1, t2    /* compute sum */
      xor    t3, t1, t2    /* if operands have different signs */
      bltz   t3, 1f        /* then overflow not possible */
      /* t1 and t2 have same sign */
      xor    t3, t0, t1    /* if sum does not also have the same sign */
      bltz   t3, L         /* then addition overflowed */
      /* nop */
   1:
```

Signed Subtraction

```
/* compute t0 = t1 - t2, branch to L on signed overflow */
      subu   t0, t1, t2    /* compute difference */
      xor    t3, t1, t2    /* if operands have same signs */
      bgez   t3, 1f        /* then overflow not possible */
      /* t1 and t2 have different signs */
      xor    t3, t0, t1    /* if difference does not also have */
                           /* the same sign as the minuend */
      bltz   t3, L         /* then subtraction overflowed */
      /* nop */
   1:
```

Unsigned Addition

```
/* compute t0 = t1 + t2 , branch to L on unsigned overflow */
      addu   t0, t1, t2
      not    t3, t1
      sltu   t3, t3, t2
      bne    t3, 0, L
```

Unsigned Subtraction

```
/* compute t0 = t1 - t2, branch to L on unsigned overflow */
      subu   t0, t1, t2
      sltu   t3, t1, t2
      bne    t3, 0, L
```

Signed Multiplication

```
/* compute t0 = t1 * t2, branch to L on signed overflow */
      mult t1, t2
      mflo t0
      mfhi t3
      sra  t4, t0, 31
      bne  t4, t3, L
```

Unsigned Multiplication

```
/* compute t0 = t1 * t2, branch to L on unsigned overflow */
      multu t1, t2
      mflo  t0
      mfhi  t3
      bne   t3, 0, L        /* if HI ≠ 0 ,then multiplication overflowed */
```

Figure C.1 Calculating Overflow for Arithmetic Operations

Multi–precision Math

Figure C.2 lists examples of routines that perform double–word addition, subtraction, and multiplication. Figure C.3 lists an example of a routine that multiplies two 64–bit values to obtain a 128–bit result.

```
#include <regdef.h>

/* Little-endian assignment of 64-bit integers to registers used. */
```

Double Word Addition

```
/* V1:V0 = A1:A0 + A3:A2 */
/* 4 instructions/cycles */
        addu    v0, a0, a2    /* add LSWs  */
        sltu    v1, v0, a0    /* set carry-in bit if add of LSWs wraps */
        addu    v1, a1        /* add in one MSW */
        addu    v1, a3        /* add in other MSW */
/* use add instead of addu for last two adds if overflow trapping desired */
```

Double Word Subtraction

```
/* V1:V0 = A1:A0 - A3:A2 */
/* 4 instructions/cycles */
        sltu    t0, a0, a2
        subu    v0, a0, a2
        subu    v1, a1, a3
        subu    v1, t0
```

Double Word Multiplication

```
/* V1:V0 = A1:A0 * A3:A2 */
/* 12 instructions, 42 cycles */
/* Note that 32-bits * 64-bits is simpler (e.g. multiply by
   small compile-time constant). */

        multu a0, a2
                /* 10 cycle interlock */
        mflo    v0
        mfhi    v1
                /* 2 nops */
        multu a1, a2
                /* 10 cycle interlock */
        mflo    t0
        addu    v1, t0
                /* 1 nop */
        multu a0, a3
                /* 10 cycle interlock */
        mflo    t0
        addu    v1, t0
```

Figure C.2 Examples of Double–Word Math Routines

```
/* Multiply 64-bit integers in t5/t4 and t7/t6 to produce 128-bit
   product in t3/t2/t1/t0.  Little-endian register order.  Destroys contents of
   a3/a2.  t5/t4 and r7/t6 unchanged.  63 cycles. */
        multu t4, t6        # x0 * y0
## 11 cycle interlock
        mflo      t0        # lo(x0 * y0)
        mfhi   t1           # hi(x0 * y0)
        not    a3, t1
## 1 nop
        multu t5, t6        # x1 * y0
## 11 cycle interlock
        mflo   a2           # lo(x1 * y0)
        mfhi   t2           # hi(x1 * y0)
        sltu   a3, a3, a2   # carry(hi(x0 * y0) + lo(x1 * y0))
        addu   t1, a2       # hi(x0 * y0) + lo(x1 * y0)
        multu t4, t7        # x0 * y1
        add    t2, a3       # hi(x1 * y0) + carry
        not    a3, t1
## 9 cycle interlock
        mflo   a2           # lo(x0 * y1)
        mfhi   t3           # hi(x0 * y1)
        sltu   a3, a3, a2   # carry((hi(x0 * y0) + lo(x1 * y0)) + lo(x0 * y1))
        addu   t1, a2       # hi(x0 * y0) + lo(x1 * y0) + lo(x0 * y1)
        multu t5, t7        # x1 * y1
        add    t2, a3       # hi(x1 * y0) + carry + carry
        not    a2, t2
        sltu   a2, a2, t3   # carry(hi(x1 * y0) + hi(x0 * y1))
        addu   t2, t3       # hi(x1 * y0) + hi(x0 * y1))
        not    a3, t2
## 6 cycle interlock
        mfhi   t3           # hi(x1 * y1)
        add    t3, a2       # hi(x1 * y1) + carry(hi(x1 * y0) + hi(x0 * y1))
        mflo   a2           # lo(x1 * y1)
        sltu   a3, a3, a2   # carry((hi(x1 * y0) + hi(x0 * y1)) + lo(x1 * y1))
        add    t3, a3
        addu   t3, a3       # hi(x1 * y0) + hi(x0 * y1) + lo(x1 * y1)
```

Figure C.3 Example of 64-bit Multiplication Routine

Double-Word Shifts

Figure C.4 illustrates examples of routines performing double word shift operations where the shift count is determined by the contents of A2.

```
/* These routines can be significantly simplified if the
   shift count is known at compile-time. */
```

Double Word Shift Left Logical

```
/* V1:V0 = A1:A0 << (A2 mod 64) */
        sll     t0, a2, 32-6
        bgez    t0, 1f
        sll     v1, a0, a2
        li      v0, 0
        b       3f
1:      sll     v1, a1, a2
        beq     t0, 0, 2f
        negu    t1, a2
        srl     t2, a0, t1
        or      v1, t2
2:      sll     v0, a0, a2
3:
```

Double Word Shift Right Logical

```
/* V1:V0 = A1:A0 >> (A2 mod 64) */
        sll     t0, a2, 32-6
        bgez    t0, 1f
        srl     v0, a1, a2
        li      v1, 0
        b       3f
1:      srl     v0, a0, a2
        beq     t0, 0, 2f
        negu    t1, a2
        sll     t2, a1, t1
        or      v0, t2
2:      srl     v1, a1, a2
3:
```

Double Word Shift Right Arithmetic

```
/* V1:V0 = A1:A0 >> (A2 mod 64) */
        sll     t0, a2, 32-6
        bgez    t0, 1f
        sra     v0, a1, a2
        sra     v1, a1, 31
        b       3f
1:      srl     v0, a0, a2
        beq     t0, 0, 2f
        negu    t1, a2
        sll     t2, a1, t1
        or      v0, t2
2:      sra     v1, a1, a2
3:
```

Figure C.4. Examples of Double-Word Shift Routines

D
Assembly Language Programming

This appendix provides an overview of the assembly language supported by the MIPS compiler system. The assembler converts assembly language statements into machine code. In most assembly languages, each instruction corresponds to a single machine instruction; however, some MIPS assembly language instructions can generate several R2000 machine instructions. This approach provides a more regular assembler that generates optimized code for certain short sequences and also results in assembly programs that can run without modification on future machines, which might have extended machine instructions. See *Basic Machine Definition* at the end of this appendix for more information about assembler instructions that generate multiple machine instructions.

Register Use and Linkage

This section describes the naming and usage conventions that the assembler applies to the R2000 and R2010 registers.

General Registers

The R2000 Processor has thirty-two 32 bit integer registers. Table D.1 summarizes the assembler's usage conventions and restrictions for these registers. The assembler reserves all register names, and you must use lowercase for the names. All register names start with a dollar sign ($).

The general registers have the names *$0..$31*. By including the file *regdef.h* (use *#include <regdef.h>*) in your program, you can use software names for some general registers. The operating system and the assembler use the general registers **$1, $26, $27, $28,** and **$29** for specific purposes. (**NOTE:** Attempts to use these general registers in other ways can produce unexpected results.) If a program uses the names **$1, $26, $27, $28, $29** rather than the names **$at, $kt0, $kt1, $gp, $sp** respectively, the assembler issues warning messages.

register name	software name (from regdef.h)	use and linkage
$0		always has the value 0
$at or $1		reserved for the assembler
$2..$3	v0–v1	used for expression evaluations and to hold integer function results. Also used to pass the static link when calling nested procedures.
$4..$7	a0–a3	used to pass the first 4 words of integer type actual arguments; their values are not preserved across procedure calls
$8..$15	t0–t7	temporary registers, used for expression evaluations; their values are not preserved across procedure calls.
$16..$23	s0–s7	saved registers; their values must be preserved across procedure calls.
$24..$25	t8–t9	temporary registers, used for expression evaluations; their values are not pre-served across procedure calls.
$26..$27 or $kt0..$kt1	k0–k1	reserved for the operating system kernel
$28 or $gp	gp	contains the global pointer
$29 or $sp	sp	contains the stack pointer
$30	s8	a saved register (like s0–s7)
$31	ra	contains the return address; used for expression evaluation.

Table D.1   General (Integer) Registers

General register **$0** always contains the value 0. All other general registers are equivalent, except that general register **$31** also serves as the implicit link register for jump and link instructions.

Special Registers

The R2000 has two 32–bit special registers. The **hi** and **lo** special registers hold the results of the multiplication (**mult** and **multu**) and division (**div** and **divu**) instructions. You usually do not need to refer explicitly to these special registers. Instructions that use the special registers refer to them automatically.

Name	Description
hi	Multiply/Divide special register holds the most significant 32 bits of multiply, remainder of divide
lo	Multiply/Divide special register holds the least significant 32 bits of multiply, quotient of divide

Floating Point Registers

The R2010 FPA has sixteen floating point registers. Each register can hold either a single precision (32 bit) or a double precision (64 bit) value. All references to these registers use an even register number (e.g., $f4). Table D.2 summarizes the assembler's usage conventions and restrictions for these registers.

register name	use and linkage
$f0..f2	used to hold floating point type function results ($f0) and complex type function results ($f0 has the real part, $f2 has the imaginary part.)
$f4..f10	temporary registers, used for expression evaluation, whose values are not preserved across procedure calls.
$f12..$f14	used to pass the first 2 single or double precision actual arguments, whose values are not preserved across procedure calls.
$f16..$f18	temporary registers, used for expression evaluations, whose values are not preserved across procedure calls.
$f20..$f30	saved registers, whose values must be preserved across procedure calls.

Table D.2 Floating Point Registers

Assembly Language Instruction Summaries

Tables D.3 through D.7 summarize the assembly language instruction set. Most of the assembly language instructions have direct machine language equivalents; refer to **Appendix A** and **Appendix B** for detailed instruction descriptions. Assembler instructions that are marked with the pointing hand symbol (☞) are synthesized by the assembler using one **or more** machine language instructions. Refer to the section *Basic Machine Definition* at the end of this appendix for a discussion of these instructions. In the tables in this appendix, the operand terms have the following meanings:

Operand	Description
destination	destination register
address	*see page D-10*
source,src1,src2	source register(s)
dest-gpr	destination register (general purpose, not coprocessor)
src-gpr	source register (general purpose, not coprocessor)
destination/src1	single register serves as both source and destination
expression	absolute value
immediate	immediate value
label	symbol label
breakcode	value that determines the break

Description	Op-code	Operand
☞ Load Address	la	destination,address
Load Byte	lb	
Load Byte Unsigned	lbu	
Load Halfword	lh	
Load Halfword Unsigned	lhu	
Load Word	lw	
Load Coprocessor z	lwcz	
Load Word Left	lwl	
Load Word Right	lwr	
Store Byte	sb	source,address
Store Halfword	sh	
Store Word	sw	
Store Word Coprocessor z	swcz	
Store Word Left	swl	
Store Word Right	swr	
☞ Unaligned Load Halfword	ulh	
☞ Unaligned Load Halfword Unsigned	ulhu	
☞ Unaligned Load Word	ulw	
☞ Unaligned Store Halfword	ush	
☞ Unaligned Store Word	usw	
Restore From Exception	rfe	
Syscall	syscall	
Break	break	breakcode
☞ No Operation	nop	

Table D.3 Load, Store and Special Instruction Summary

Description	Op-code	Operand
☞ Load Immediate Load Upper Immediate	li lui	destination,expression
☞ Absolute Value ☞ Negate (with overflow) ☞ Negate (without overflow) ☞ NOT	abs neg negu not	destination,src1 destination/src1
Add (with overflow) Add (without overflow) AND ☞ Divide (with overflow) ☞ Divide (without overflow) EXCLUSIVE OR ☞ Multiply ☞ Multiply (with overflow) ☞ Multiply (with overflow) Unsigned NOT OR OR ☞ Remainder ☞ Remainder Unsigned ☞ Rotate Left ☞ Rotate Right ☞ Set Equal Set Less Than Set Less Than Unsigned ☞ Set Less/Equal ☞ Set Less/Equal Unsigned ☞ Set Greater Than ☞ Set Greater Than Unsigned ☞ Set Greater/Equal ☞ Set Greater/Equal Unsigned ☞ Set Not Equal Shift Left Logical Shift Right Arithmetic Shift Right Logical Subtract (with overflow) Subtract (without overflow)	add addu and div divu xor mul mulo mulou nor or rem remu rol ror seq slt sltu sle sleu sgt sgtu sge sgeu sne sll sra srl sub subu	destination,src1,src2 destination/src1,src2 destination,src1,immediate destination/src1,immediate
Multiply Multiply Unsigned	mult multu	src1,src2

Table D.4 Computational Instruction Summary

Description	Op-code	Operand
Branch Branch Coprocessor z True Branch Coprocessor z False	**b** **b**c**z t** **b**c**z f**	label
Branch on Equal ☞Branch on Greater ☞Branch on Greater/Equal ☞Branch on Greater/Equal Unsigned ☞Branch on Greater Than Unsigned ☞Branch on Less ☞Branch on Less/Equal ☞Branch on Less/Equal Unsigned ☞Branch on Less Than Unsigned Branch on Not Equal	**beq** **bgt** **bge** **bgeu** **bgtu** **blt** **ble** **bleu** **bltu** **bne**	src1,src2,label src1,immediate,label
Branch and Link	**bal**	label
Branch on Equal Zero Branch on Greater/Equal Zero Branch on Greater or Equal to Zero And Link Branch on Greater Than Zero Branch on Less/Equal Zero Branch on Less Than Zero Branch on Less Than Zero And Link Branch on Not Equal Zero	**beqz** **bgez** **bgezal** **bgtz** **blez** **bltz** **bltzal** **bnez**	src1,label
Jump Jump And Link	**j** **jal**	address src1
Coprocessor z Operation	**c**z	expression
☞Move	**move**	destination,src1
Move From HI Register Move To HI Register Move From LO Register Move To LO Register	**mfhi** **mthi** **mflo** **mtlo**	register
Move From Coprocessor z Move To Coprocessor z	**mfc**z **mtc**z	dest–gpr, source src–gpr, destination
Control From Coprocessor z Control To Coprocessor z	**cfc**z **ctc**z	src–gpr, destination dest–gpr, source
Translation Lookaside Buffer Probe Translation Lookaside Buffer Read Translation Lookaside Buffer Write Random Translation Lookaside Write Index	**tlbp** **tlbr** **tlbwr** **tlbwi**	

Table D.5 Jump, Branch and Coprocessor Instruction Summary

Description	Op-code	Operand
Load Fp Double Single	l.d l.s	destination,address
Store Fp Double Single	s.d s.s	source,address
Move Fp Single Double	mov.s mov.d	destination,src1
Absolute Value Fp Double Single	abs.d abs.s	destination,src1
Add Fp Double Single **Divide Fp** Double Single **Multiply Fp** Double Single **Subtract Fp** Double Single	add.d add.s dlv.d div.s mul.d mul.s sub.d sub.s	destination,src1,src2
Convert Source to **Specified Precision Fp** Double to Single Fixed Point to Single Fixed Point to Double Single to Double Double to Fixed Point Single to Fixed Point	cvt.s.d cvt.s.w cvt.d.w cvt.d.s cvt.w.d cvt.w.s	destination,src2
Negate Floating Point Double Single	neg.d neg.s	destination,src2

Table D.6 Floating Point Instruction Summary

Description	Op-code	Operand
Compare Fp		
F Single	c.f.s	src1,src2
F Double	c.f.d	
UN Single	c.un.s	
UN Double	c.un.d	
*EQ Single	c.eq.s	
*EQ Double	c.eq.d	
UEQ Single	c.ueq.s	
UEQ Double	c.ueq.d	
OLT Single	c.olt.s	
OLT Double	c.olt.d	
ULT Single	c.ult.s	
ULT Double	c.ult.d	
OLE Single	c.ole.s	
OLE Double	c.ole.d	
ULE Single	c.ule.s	
ULE Double	c.ule.d	
SF Single	c.sf.s	
SF Double	c.sf.d	
NGLE Single	c.ngle.s	
NGLE Double	c.ngle.d	
SEQ Single	c.deq.s	
SEQ Double	c.seq.d	
NGL Single	c.ngl.s	
NGL Double	c.ngl.d	
*LT Single	c.lt.s	
*LT Double	c.lt.d	
NGE Single	c.nge.s	
NGE Double	c.nge.d	
*LE Single	c.le.s	
*LE Double	c.le.d	
NGT Single	c.ngt.s	
NGT Double	c.ngt.d	

* These are the most common Compare instructions. The other Compare instructions are provided for IEEE compatibility.

Table D.7 Floating Point Compare Instruction Summary

Addressing

This section describes the formats that you can use to specify addresses. Access to halfwords requires alignment on even byte boundaries, and access to words requires alignment on byte boundaries that are divisible by four. Any attempt to address a data item that does not have the proper alignment causes an alignment exception.

The unaligned assembler load and store instructions may generate multiple machine language instructions. They do not raise alignment exceptions. These instructions load and store unaligned data:

- load word left (lwl)
- load word right (lwr)
- store word left (swl)
- store word right (swr)
- unaligned load word (ulw)
- unaligned load halfword (ulh)
- unaligned load halfword unsigned (ulhu)
- unaligned store word (usw)
- unaligned store halfword (ush)

These instructions load and store aligned data:

- load word (lw)
- load halfword (lh)
- load halfword unsigned (lhu)
- load byte (lb)
- load byte unsigned (lbu)
- store word (sw)
- store halfword (sh)
- store byte (sb)

Address Formats

The R2000 Processor supports only one addressing mode — base register plus a signed 16-bit offset. The assembler, however, synthesizes some additional addressing modes to present more traditional addressing capabilities to the assembly language programmer. The assembler accepts these formats for addresses:

Format	Address
(base register)	base address (zero offset assumed)
expression	absolute address
expression (base register)	based address
relocatable-symbol	relocatable address
relocatable-symbol ± expression	relocatable address
relocatable-symbol ± expression (index register)	indexed relocatable address

Each of these addressing formats is described in the table that follows.

Address Descriptions

Expression	Address Description
(base-register)	Specifies an indexed address, which assumes a zero offset. The base-register's contents specify the address.
expression	Specifies an absolute address. The assembler generates the most locally efficient code for referencing a value at the specified address.
expression (base-register)	Specifies a based address. To get the address, the machine adds the value of the expression to the contents of the base-register.
relocatable-symbol	Specifies a relocatable address. The assembler generates the necessary instruction(s) to address the item and generates relocatable information for the link editor.
relocatable-symbol ± expression	Specifies a relocatable address. To get the address, the assembler adds or subtracts the value of the expression, which has an absolute value, from the relocatable symbol. The assembler generates the necessary instruction(s) to address the item and generates relocatable information for the link editor. If the symbol name does not appear as a label anywhere in the assembly, the assembler assumes that the symbol is external.
relocatable-symbol (index-register)	Specifies an indexed relocatable address. To get the address, the machine adds the index-register to the relocatable symbol's address. The assembler generates the necessary instruction(s) to address the item and generates relocatable information for the link editor. If the symbol name does not appear as a label anywhere in the assembly, the assembler assumes that the symbol is external.
relocatable-symbol ± expression (index-register)	Specifies an indexed relocatable address. To get the address, the assembler adds or subtracts the relocatable symbol, the expression, and the contents of the index-register. The assembler generates the necessary instruction(s) to address the item and generates relocation information for the link editor. If the symbol does not appear as a label anywhere in the assembly, the assembler assumes that the symbol is external.

Pseudo Op–Codes

The keywords in this section describe pseudo op–codes (directives). These pseudo op–codes influence the assembler's later behavior. In the text, boldface type specifies a keyword and italics represents an operand that you define.

Pseudo–Op	Description
.align *expression*	Advance the location counter to make the *expression* low order bits of the counter zero.
	Normally, the **.half**, **.word**, **.float**, and **.double** directives automatically align their data appropriately. For example, **.word** does an implicit **.align 2** (**.double** does a **.align 3**). You disable the automatic alignment feature with **.align 0**. The assembler reinstates automatic alignment at the next **.text**, **.data**, **.rdata**, or **.sdata** directive.
	Labels immediately preceding an automatic or explicit alignment are also realigned. For example, foo: .align 3; .word 0 is the same as **.align ; foo: .word 0** .
.ascii *string [, string]...*	Assembles each *string* from the list into successive locations. The **.ascii** directive does not null pad the string. You MUST put quotation marks (") around each string. You can use the C language backslash escape characters.
asciiz *string [, string]...*	Assembles each *string* in the list into successive locations and adds a null. You can use the C language backslash escape characters.
.asm0	(For use by compilers.) Tells the assembler's second pass that this assembly came from the assembler's first pass.
.bgnb *symno*	(For use by compilers.) Sets the beginning of a language block. The **.bgnb** and **.endb** directives delimit the scope of a variable set. The scope can be an entire procedure, or it can be a nested scope (for example a "{}" block in the C language). The symbol number *symno* refers to a dense number in a **.T** file. For an explanation of **.T** files, see the *MIPS Languages Programmer's Guide*. To set the end of a language block, see **.endb**.
.byte *expression1 [, expression2]...[, expressionN]*	Truncates the *expressions* from the comma–separated list to 8-bit values, and assembles the values in successive locations. The *expression*s must be absolute. The operands can optionally have the form: *expressionVal* : *expressionRep*. The *expressionRep* replicates *expressionVal*'s value *expressionRep* times.

Pseudo–Op	Description
.comm *name, expression*	Unless defined elsewhere, *name* becomes a global common symbol at the head of a block of *expression* bytes of storage. The linker overlays like–named common blocks, using the maximum of the *expression*s.
.data	Tells the assembler to add all subsequent data to the **data** section.
.double *expression [, expression2] ...[, expressionN]*	Initializes memory to 64–bit floating point numbers. The operands can optionally have the form: *expressionVal* [: *expressionRep*]. The *expressionVal* is the floating point value. The optional *expressionRep* is a non–negative expression that specifies a repetition count. The *expressionRep* replicates *expressionVal*'s value *expressionRep* times. This directive automatically aligns its data and any preceding labels to a double–word boundary. You can disable this feature by using **.align 0**.
.end *[proc_name]*	Sets the end of a procedure. Use this directive when you want to generate information for the debugger. To set the beginning of a procedure, see **.ent**.
.endb *symno*	(For use by compilers.) Sets the end of a language block. To set the beginning of a language block, see **.bgnb**.
.endr	Signals the end of a repeat block. To start a repeat block, see **.repeat**.
.ent *proc_name*	Sets the beginning of the procedure *proc_name*. Use this directive when you want to generate information for the debugger. To set the end of a procedure, see **.end**.
.extern *name expression*	*name* is a global undefined symbol whose size is assumed to be *expression* bytes. The advantage of using this directive, instead of permitting an undefined symbol to become global by default, is that the assembler can decide whether to use the economical $gp–relative addressing mode, depending on the value of the –G option. As a special case, if *expression* is zero, the assembler refrains from using $gp to address this symbol regardless of the size specified by –G.
.err	(For use by compilers.) Signals an error. Any compiler front–end that detects an error condition puts this directive in the input stream. When the assembler encounters a .err, it quietly ceases to assemble the source file. This prevents the assembler from continuing to process a program that is incorrect.
.file *file_number file_name string*	(For use by compilers.) Specifies the source file corresponding to the assembly instructions that follow.

Pseudo-Op	Description

.float *expression1* [, *expression2*]... [, *expressionN*]

Initializes memory to single precision 32-bit floating point numbers. The operands can optionally have the form: *expressionVal* [: *expressionRep*]. The optional *expressionRep* is a non-negative expression that specifies a repetition count. This optional form replicates *expressionVal*'s value *expressionRep* times. This directive automatically aligns its data and preceding labels to a word boundary. You can disable this feature by using **.align 0**.

.fmask *mask, offset*

(For use by compilers.) Sets a mask with a bit turned on for each floating point register that the current routine saved. The least-significant bit corresponds to register **$f0**. The offset is the distance in bytes from the virtual frame pointer at which the floating point registers are saved. The assembler saves higher register numbers closer to the virtual frame pointer. You must use **.ent** before **.fmask** and only one **.fmask** may be used per **.ent**. Space should be allocated for those registers specified in the **.fmask**.

.frame *frame-register, offset, return_pc_register*

Describes a stack frame. The first register is the frame-register, the offset is the distance from the frame register to the virtual frame pointer, and the second register is the return program counter (or, if the first register is **$0**, this directive shows that the return program counter is saved four bytes from the virtual frame pointer). You must use **.ent** before **.frame** and only one **.frame** may be used per **.ent**. No stack traces can be done in the debugger without **.frame**.

.globl *name*

Makes the *name* external. If the name is otherwise defined (by its appearance as a label), the assembler will export the symbol; otherwise it will import the symbol. In general, the assembler imports undefined symbols (that is, it gives them the UNIX storage class "global undefined" and requires the linker to resolve them).

.half *expression1* [, *expression2*] ... [, *expressionN*]

Truncates the *expression*s in the comma-separated list to 16-bit values and assembles the values in successive locations. The *expression*s must be absolute. This directive can optionally have the form: *expressionVal* [: *expressionRep*]. The *expressionRep* replicates *expressionVal*'s value *expressionRep* times. This directive automatically aligns its data appropriately. You can disable this feature by using **.align 0**.

.lab *label_name*

(For use by compilers). Associates a named label with the current location in the program text.

Pseudo–Op	Description
.lcomm *name, expression*	Makes the *name*'s data type **bss**. The assembler allocates the named symbol to the **bss** area, and the expression defines the named symbol's length. If a **.globl** directive also specifies the name, the assembler allocates the named symbol to external **bss**. The assembler puts **bss** symbols in one of two **bss** areas. If the defined size is smaller than the size specified by the assembler or compiler's –G command line option, the assembler puts the symbols in the **sbss** area and uses **$gp** to address the data.
.loc *file_number line_number*	(For use by compilers). Specifies the source file and the line within that file that corresponds to the assembly instructions that follow. The assembler ignores the file number when this directive appears in the assembly source file. Then, the assembler assumes that the directive refers to the most recent .**file** directive. When a .**loc** directive appears in the binary assembly language .**G** file, the file number is a dense number pointing at a file symbol in the symbol table .**T** file. For more information about .**G** and .**T** files, see the *Languages Programmer's Guide*.
.mask *mask, offset*	(For use by compilers.) Sets a mask with a bit turned on for each general purpose register that the current routine saved. Bit one corresponds to register **$1**. The offset is the distance in bytes from the virtual frame pointer where the registers are saved. The assembler saves higher register numbers closer to the the virtual frame pointer. Space should be allocated for those registers appearing in the mask. If bit zero is set it is assumed that space is allocated for all 31 registers regardless of whether they appear in the mask.
nop	Tells the assembler to put in an instruction that has no effect on the machine state. While several instructions cause no–operation, the assembler only considers the ones generated by the **nop** directive to be wait instructions. This directive puts an explicit delay in the instruction stream.
.option *options*	(For use by compilers). Tells the assembler that certain options were in effect during compilation. (These options can, for example, limit the assembler's freedom to perform branch optimizations.) This option is intended for compiler–generated .s files rather than for hand–coded ones.
.repeat *expression*	Repeats all instructions or data between the .**repeat** directive and the .**endr** directive. The *expression* defines how many times the data repeats. With the .**repeat** directive, you CANNOT use labels, branch instructions, or values that require relocation in the block. To end a .**repeat**, see .**endr**.

Pseudo–Op	Description
.rdata	Tells the assembler to add subsequent data into the **rdata** section.
.sdata	Tells the assembler to add subsequent data to the **sdata** section.
.set *option*	Instructs the assembler to enable or to disable certain options. Use set options only for hand–crafted assembly routines. The assembler has these default options: **reorder, macro,** and **at.** You can specify only one option for each .set directive. You can specify these .set options:

- The **reorder** option lets the assembler reorder machine language instructions to improve performance.

- The **noreorder** option prevents the assembler from reordering machine language instructions. If a machine language instruction violates the hardware pipeline constraints, the assembler issues a warning message.

- The **macro** option lets the assembler generate multiple machine instructions from a single assembler instruction.

- The **nomacro** option causes the assembler to print a warning whenever an assembler operation generates more than one machine language instruction. You must select the **noreorder** option before using the **nomacro** option; otherwise, an error results.

- The **at** option lets the assembler use the **$at** register for macros, but generates warnings if the source program uses **$at**.

- When you use the **noat** option and an assembler operation requires the **$at** register, the assembler issues a warning message; however, the **noat** option does let source programs use **$at** without issuing warnings.

- The **nomove** options tells the assembler to mark each subsequent instruction so that it cannot be moved during reorganization. Because the assembler can still insert nop instructions where necessary for pipeline constraints, this option is less stringent than **noreorder.** The assembler can still move instructions from below the **nomove** region to fill delay slots above the region or vice versa. The **nomove** option has part of the effect of the "volatile" C declaration; it prevents otherwise independent loads or stores from occurring in a different order than intended.

- The **move** option cancels the effect of **nomove.**

Pseudo–Op	Description
.space *expression*	Advances the location counter by the value of the specified *expression* bytes. The assembler fills the space with zeros.
.struct *expression*	This permits you to lay out a structure using labels plus directives like .**word,** .**byte,** and so forth. It ends at the next segment directive (.**data,** .**text,** etc.). It does not emit any code or data, but defines the labels within it to have values which are the sum of *expression* plus their offsets from the .**struct** itself.

Pseudo-Op	Description
(symbolic equate)	Takes one of these forms: *name = expression* or *name = register*. You must define the name only once in the assembly, and you CANNOT redefine the name. The expression must be computable when you assemble the program, and the expression must involve operators, constants, and equated symbols. You can use the name as a constant in any later statement.
.text	Tells the assembler to add subsequent code to the **text** section. (This is the default.)
.verstamp *major minor*	(For use by compilers.) Specifies the major and minor version numbers (for example, version 0.15 would be **.verstamp** 0 15).
.vreg *register offset symno*	(For use by compilers.) Describes a register variable by giving the offset from the virtual frame pointer and the symbol number *symno* (the dense number) of the surrounding procedure.
.word *expression1* [, *expression2*] ... [, *expressionN*]	Truncates the *expressions* in the comma–separated list to 32 bits and assembles the values in successive locations. The *expressions* must be absolute. The operands can optionally have the form: *expressionVal* [: *expressionRep*]. The *expressionRep* replicates *expressionVal*'s value *expressionRep* times. This directive automatically aligns its data and preceding labels to a word boundary. You can disable this feature by using **.align 0**.

Linkage Conventions

This section gives rules and examples to follow when designing an assembly language program. When you write assembly language routines, you should follow the same calling conventions that the compilers observe, for two reasons:

- Often your code must interact with compiler–generated code, accepting and returning arguments or accessing shared global data.

- The symbolic debugger gives better assistance in debugging programs using standard calling conventions.

The conventions for the MIPS compiler system are a bit more complicated than some. This complexity is needed mostly to enhance the speed of each procedure call. Specifically:

- The compilers use the full, general calling sequence only when necessary; where possible, they omit unneeded portions of it. For example, the compilers avoid using a register as a frame pointer whenever possible.

- The compilers and debugger observe certain implicit rules rather than communicating via instructions or data at execution time. For example, the debugger looks at information placed in the symbol table by a ".frame" directive at compilation time, so that it can tolerate the lack of a register containing a frame pointer at execution time.

Program Design

This section describes two general areas of concern to the assembly language programmer:

- stack frame requirements on entering and exiting a routine

- register usage and restrictions

The Stack Frame

The compilers classify each routine into one of the following categories:

- non–leaf routines; that is, routines that call some other routines

- leaf routines; that is, routines that do not themselves execute any procedure calls. Leaf routines are of two types:

○ leaf routines that require stack storage for local variables

○ leaf routines that do not require stack storage for local variables.

You must decide the routine category before determining the calling sequence.

To write a program with proper stack frame usage and debugging capabilities, use the following procedure:

1. *PROLOG* Regardless of the type of routine, you should include a **.ent** pseudo-op and an entry label for the procedure. The **.ent** pseudo-op is for use by the debugger, and the entry label is the procedure name. The syntax is:

   ```
         .ent procedure_name
   procedure_name:
   ```

2. If you are writing a leaf procedure that does not use the stack, skip to step 3. For leaf procedure that uses the stack or non-leaf procedures, you must allocate all the stack space that the routine requires. The syntax to adjust the stack size is:

   ```
   subu $sp,framesize
   ```

   where *framesize* is the size of frame required. Space must be allocated for:

   • local variables

   • saved general registers. Space should be allocated only for those registers saved. For non-leaf procedures, you must save $31, which is used in the calls to other procedures from this routine. If you use registers $16–$23 or $30, you must also save them.

   • saved floating point registers. Space should be allocated only for those registers saved. If you use registers $f20–$f30 you must also save them.

   • Procedure call argument area. You must allocate the maximum number of bytes for arguments of any procedure that you call from this routine.

   NOTE: Once you have modified $sp, you should not modify it again for the rest of the routine (unless you are using a non-virtual frame pointer).

3. Now include a **.frame** pseudo-op:

   ```
   .frame          framereg,framesize,returnreg
   ```

The virtual frame pointer is a frame pointer as used in other compiler systems but has no register allocated for it. It consists of the *framereg* ($sp, in most cases) added to the *framesize* (see step 2 above). Figure D.1 illustrates the stack components.

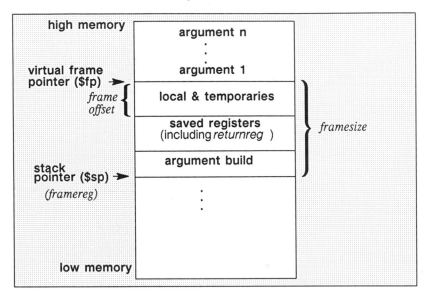

Figure D.1 Stack Organization

The *returnreg* specifies the register the return address is in (usually $31). These usual values may change if you use a varying stack pointer or are specifying a kernel trap routine.

4. If the procedure is a leaf procedure that does not use the stack, skip to step 5. Otherwise you must save the registers you allocated space for in step 2.

   To save the general registers, use the following operations:

```
.mask      bitmask,frameoffset
sw         reg,framesize+frameoffset-N($sp)
```

The **.mask** directive specifies the registers to be stored and where they are stored. A bit should be on in *bitmask* for each register saved. For example, if register $31 is saved, bit 31 should be '1' in *bitmask*. Bits are set in bitmask in little–endian order, even if the machine configuration is big-endian. The *frameoffset* is the offset from the virtual frame pointer (this number is usually negative). *N* should be 0 for the highest numbered register saved and then incremented by four for each subsequently lower numbered register saved. For example:

```
sw     $31,framesize+frameoffset($sp)
sw     $17,framesize+frameoffset-4($sp)
sw     $16,framesize+frameoffset-8($sp)
```

Figure D.2 illustrates this example.

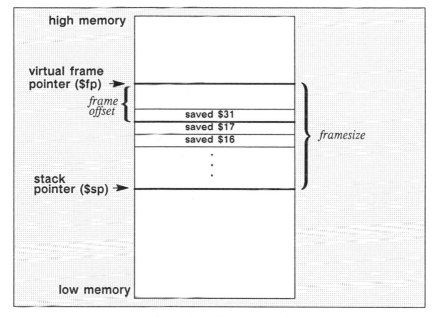

Figure D.2   Stack Example

Now save any floating point registers that you allocated space for in step 2 as follows:

```
.fmask    bitmask,frameoffset
s.[sd]    reg,framesize+frameoffset-N($sp)
```

Notice that saving floating point registers is identical to saving general registers except we use the **.fmask** pseudo-op instead of **.mask**, and the stores are of floating point singles or doubles. The discussion regarding saving general registers applies here as well, but remember that *N* should be incremented by 8 for doubles.

5. This step describes parameter passing: how to access arguments passed into your routine and passing arguments correctly to other procedures. For information on high–level language specific constructs (call–by–name, call–by–value, string or structure passing), refer to Chapter 3 of the *MIPS Language Programmer's Guide*.

   As specified in step 2, space must be allocated on the stack for all arguments even though they may be passed in registers. This provides a saving area if their registers are needed for other variables.

   General registers $4–$7 and floating point registers $f12, $f14 must be used for passing the first two arguments (if possible). You must allocate a pair of registers (even if it's a single precision argument) that start with an even register for floating point arguments appearing in registers.

   In the table below, the 'fN' arguments are considered single or double precision floating point arguments, and 'nN' arguments are everything else. The elipses (...) mean that the rest of the arguments do not go in registers regardless of their type. The 'stack' assignment means that you do not put this argument in a register. The register assignments occur in the order shown in order to satisfy optimizing compiler protocols.

Arguments	Register Assignments
(f1, f2, ...)	f1 –> $f12, f2 –> $f14
(f1, n1, f2, ...)	f1 –> $f12, n1 –> $6, f2 –> stack
(f1, n1, n2, ...)	f1 –> $f12, n1 –> $6, n2 –> $7
(n1, n2, n3, n4, ...)	n1 –> $4, n2 –> $5, n3 –> $6, n4 –> $7
(n1, n2, n3, f1, ...)	n1 –> $4, n2 –> $5, n3 –> $6, f1 –> stack
(n1, n2, f1, ...)	n1 –> $4, n2 –> $5, f1 –> ($6, $7)
(n1, f1, ...)	n1 –> $4, f1 –> ($6, $7)

6. *EPILOG* Next, you must restore registers that were saved in step 4. To restore general purpose registers:

        lw   reg,framesize+frameoffset–N($sp)

   To restore the floating point registers:

        l.[sd]   reg,framesize+frameoffset–N($sp)

(Refer to step 4 for a discussion of the value of *N*.)

7. Get the return address:

```
lw    $31,framesize+frameoffset($sp)
```

8. Clean up the stack:

```
addu $sp, framesize
```

9. Return:

```
j    $31
```

10. To end the procedure:

```
.end procedurename
```

Examples

This section contains the examples that illustrate program design rules; each example shows a procedure written in the C language and its equivalent written in assembly language.

Figure D.3 shows a non–leaf procedure. Notice that it creates a stackframe, and also saves its return address since it must put a new return address into register $31 when it invokes its callee:

```
float
nonleaf(i, j)
  int i, *j;
  {
  double atof();
  int temp;

  temp = i - *j;
  if (i < *j) temp = -temp;
  return atof(temp);
  }
```

```
                .globl   nonleaf           ## define nonleaf as external
#     1         float
#     2         nonleaf(i, j)
#     3           int i, *j;
#     4           {
                .ent     nonleaf           ## tell debugger this starts nonleaf
nonleaf:                                   ## this is the entry point
                subu     $sp, 24           ## Create stackframe
                sw       $31, 20($sp)      ## Save the return address
                .mask    0x80000000, -4    ## only $31 was saved at ($sp)+24-4
                .frame   $sp, 24, $31      ## define frame size, return reg.
#     5           double atof();
#     6           int temp;
#     7
#     8           temp = i - *j;
                lw       $2, 0($5)         ## Arguments are in $4 and $5
                subu     $3, $4, $2
#     9           if (i < *j) temp = -temp;
                bge      $4, $2, $32       ## Note: $32 is a label, not a register
                negu     $3, $3
$32:
#    10           return atof(temp);
                move     $4, $3
                jal      atof
                cvt.s.d  $f0, $f0          ## Return value goes in $f0
                lw       $31, 20($sp)      ## Restore return address
                addu     $sp, 24           ## Delete stackframe
                j        $31               ## Return to caller
                .end     nonleaf           ## Mark end of nonleaf
```

Figure D.3   Non–Leaf Procedure

Figure D.4 shows a leaf procedure that does not require stack space for local variables. Notice that it creates no stackframe, and saves no return address:

```
int
leaf(pl, p2)
  int pl, p2;
  {
  return (pl > p2) ? pl : p2;
  }

              .globl        leaf
#    1        int
#    2        leaf(pl, p2)
#    3          int pl, p2;
#    4          {
              .ent          leaf
leaf:
              .frame        $sp, 0, $31
#    5          return (pl > p2) ? pl : p2;
              ble           $4, $5, $32      ## Arguments in $4 and $5
              move          $3, $4
              b             $33
$32:
              move          $3, $5
$33:
              move          $2, $3           ## Return value goes in $2
              j             #31              ## Return to caller
#    6          }
              .end    leaf
```

Figure D.4 Leaf Procedure Without Stack Space for Local Variables

Figure D.5 shows a leaf procedure that requires stack space for local variables. Notice that it creates a stack frame, but does not save a return address.

```
char
leaf_storage(i)
  int i;
  {
  char a[16];
  int j;

  for (j = 0; j < 10; j++)
    a[j] = '0' + j;
  for (j = 10; j < 16; j++)
    a[j] = 'a' + j;
  return a[i];
  }
            .globl  leaf_storage      ##
#    1      char
#    2      leaf_storage(i)
#    3        int i;
#    4        {
            .ent    leaf_storage 2   ## "2" is the lexical level of the
leaf_storage:                        ## procedure.  You may omit it.
            subu    $sp, 24          ## Create stackframe
            .frame  $sp, 24, $31
#    5        char a[16];
#    6        int j;
#    7
#    8        for (j = 0; j < 10; j++)
            sw      $0, 4($sp)
            addu    $3, $sp, 24
$32:
#    9        a[j] = '0' + j;
            lw      $14, 4($sp)
            addu    $15, $14, 48
            addu    $24, $3, $14
            sb      $15, -16($24)
            lw      $25, 4($sp)
            addu    $8, $25, 1
            sw      $8, 4($sp)
            blt     $8, 10, $32
#   10        for (j = 10; j < 16; j++)
            li      $9, 10
            sw      $9, 4($sp)
$33:
#   11        a[j] = 'a' + j;
            lw      $10, 4($sp)
            addu    $11, $10, 97
            addu    $12, $3, $10
            sb      $11, -16($12)
            lw      $13, 4($sp)
            addu    $14, $13, 1
            sw      $14, 4($sp)
            blt     $14, 16, $33
#   12        return a[i];
            addu    $15, $3, $4       ## Argument is in $4
            lbu     $2, -16($15)      ## Return value goes in $2
            addu    $sp, 24          ## Delete stackframe
            j       $31              ## Return to caller
            .end    leaf_storage     ##
```

Figure D.5 *Leaf Procedure with Stack Space for Local Variables*

Memory Allocation

The system's default memory allocation scheme gives every process two storage areas that can grow without bound. A process exceeds virtual storage only when the sum of the two areas exceeds virtual storage space. The link editor and assembler use the scheme shown in Figure D.6

0xffffffff	**Reserved for Kernel** (accessible from Kernel mode) **(2GB)**	
0x8fffffff 0x7fffffff	**Not Accessible** (by convention, not a hardware implementation) **(4KB)**	Reserved for operating system use
0x7ffff000		
0x7fffefff $sp ➤	**Activation Stack** (grows toward zero)	Used for local data in C programs
	Protected (grows from either edge)	Allocated as requested by users (as in System V shared memory regions)
	Heap (grows upward)	Reserved for sbrk and break system calls. Not always present.
	.bss	Used for local data (block started by storage)
	.sbss	Small bss section
$gp ➤	**.sdata**	Small data section
	.data	Data section
0x10000000	**.rdata**	Read-only data section
0xfffffff	**Reserved for Shared Libraries**	
	Not Used	
0x400000	**Program .text** (including header)	
0x3fffff 0x0	**Reserved** **(4MB)**	

Figure D.6 Memory Layout (User Program View)

Basic Machine Definition

The assembly language instructions are a superset of the actual R2000's machine instructions. Generally, the assembly language instructions match the machine instructions; however, in some cases the assembly language instructions are macros that generate more than one machine instruction (the assembly language multiplication instructions are examples).

You can, in most instances, consider the assembly instructions as machine instructions; however, for routines that require tight coding for performance reasons, you must be aware of the assembly instructions that generate more than one machine language instruction, as described in this section.

Load and Store Instructions

If you use an *address* as an operand in an assembler **Load** or **Store** instruction and the address references a data item that is not addressable through register **$gp** or the data item does not have an absolute address in the range **−32768...32767**, the assembler instruction generates a **lui** (load upper immediate) machine instruction and generates the appropriate offset to **$at**. The assembler then uses **$at** as the index address for the reference. This condition occurs when the address has a relocatable external name offset (or index) from where the offset began.

The assembler's **la** (load address) instruction generates an **addiu** (add unsigned immediate) machine instruction. If the address requires it, the **la** instruction also generates a **lui** (load upper immediate) machine instruction. The machine requires the **la** instruction because **la** couples relocatable information with the instruction for symbolic addresses.

Depending on the expression's value, the assembler's **li** (load immediate) instruction can generate one or two machine instructions. For values in the **−32768...65535** range or for values that have zeros as the 16 least significant bits, the **li** instruction generates a single machine instruction; otherwise it generates two machine instructions.

Computational Instructions

If a computational instruction immediate value falls outside the **0...65535** range for Logical ANDs, Logical ORs, or Logical XORs (exclusive or), the immediate field causes the machine to explicitly load a constant to a temporary register. Other instructions generate a single machine instruction when a value falls in the **−32768...32767** range.

The assembler's **seq** (set equal) and **sne** (set not equal) instructions generate three machine instructions each.

If one operand is a literal outside the range −32768...32767, the assembler's **sge** (set greater than or equal to) and **sle** (set less/equal) instructions generate two machine instructions each.

The assembler's **mulo** and **mulou** (multiply) instructions generate machine instructions to test for overflow and to move the result to a general register; if the destination register is **$0**, the check and move are not generated.

The assembler's **mul** (multiply unsigned) instruction generates a machine instruction to move the result to a general register; if the destination register is **$0**, the move and overflow checking is not generated. The assembler's divide instructions, **div** (divide with overflow) and **divu** (divide without overflow), generate machine instructions to check for division by zero and to move the quotient into a general register; if the destination register is **$0**, the move is not generated.

The assembler's **rem** (signed) and **remu** (unsigned) instructions also generate multiple instructions.

The rotate instructions **ror** (rotate right) and **rol** (rotate left) generate three machine instructions each.

The **abs** (absolute value) instruction generates three machine instructions.

Branch Instructions

If the immediate value is not zero, the branch instructions **beq** (branch on equal) and **bne** (branch on not equal), each generate a load literal machine instruction. The relational instructions generate a **slt** (**set less than**) machine instruction to determine whether one register is less than or greater than another. Relational instructions can reorder the operands and branch on either zero or not zero as required to do an operation.

Coprocessor Instructions

For symbolic addresses, the coprocessor interface **Load** and **Store** instructions, **lwcz** (load coprocessor z) and **swcz** (store coprocessor z) can generate a **lui** (load upper immediate) machine instruction.

Special Instructions

The assembler's **break** instruction packs the **breakcode** operand in unused register fields. An operating system convention determines the position.

IEEE Floating–Point Standard Compatibility Issues

MIPS has defined a floating–point coprocessor architecture that can be implemented using various combinations of hardware and software. The main body of this manual describes the functions of the architecture implemented by the R2010 FPA. When the FPA is used in conjunction with the UMIPS operating system, the resulting architecture fully conforms to the requirements of ANSI/IEEE Standard 754–1985, IEEE Standard for Binary Floating–Point Arithmetic. In addition to conforming to the requirements of the IEEE standard, the MIPS floating–point coprocessor architecture fully supports the standard's recommendations. In certain fairly obscure cases, the IEEE standard's recommendations are incomplete, ambiguous, or left to the implementors' discretion. The following section describes the interpretations chosen for the MIPS floating–point architecture. Subsequent sections briefly describe the software support that the FPA requires in order to meet the standard's recommendations.

Interpretation of the Standard

The sections that follow describe how the MIPS architecture interprets those parts of the standard that are left up to the implementor.

Underflow

The IEEE standard gives the implementor choices in the detection of underflow conditions. The MIPS floating–point architecture requires that tininess be detected after rounding, and that loss of accuracy be detected as inexact result.

Exceptions

The IEEE standard does not define, when an exception condition occurs, how the exception field is set when traps are disabled, or how the sticky exception field is set when traps are enabled. The MIPS floating–point architecture requires that the exception field be loaded (set or cleared), and that the sticky exception field be set, regardless of whether traps are enabled.

Inexact

The IEEE standard specifies that an inexact exception may occur concurrently with an overflow or underflow exception, and that the overflow or underflow exception trap take priority. It further requires that the inexact trap be taken when an operation overflows while the overflow trap is disabled. The MIPS floating–point architecture specifies that both the inexact exception and the overflow or underflow exception are signaled in these cases. A floating–point trap occurs if either exception is enabled; software is responsible for passing control to the appropriate trap handler.

NaNs

The IEEE standard specifies that a quiet NaN be generated when an invalid operation occurs with the exception trap disabled, but does not further specify the value generated. The MIPS floating–point architecture specifies that in such cases, the NaN generated shall have a mantissa field of all ones, except for the high–order fractional significand bit. The sign bit shall be positive, and the explicit integer bit, if present, shall be set. If the result is a fixed–point integer format, the largest positive value is generated instead. When the invalid operation exception occurs due to one or more of the operands being signaling NaNs, a new quiet NaN is generated according to the rules above. These values are listed in the following table:

Format	Generated NaN value
single	7fbfffff
double	7ff7ffff ffffffff
word	7fffffff

Software Assistance for IEEE Standard Compatibility

The standard does not require that all floating–point operations be performed in high–performance hardware, and it does not specify the instruction-set presentation. Therefore, when little performance advantage is realized by performing an operation in hardware, the MIPS architecture has simplified the hardware (the FPA) and requires that the operation be performed using software assistance. Operations which occur with low dynamic frequency may then be implemented in software, while still providing hardware implementations of frequent operations.

The most complex part of the IEEE standard involves fully supporting the required and recommended exceptional conditions that arise in floating–point computation, such as overflow, underflow, and invalid operation. Here again, the MIPS architecture employs exception traps, when applicable, to relieve the FPA from handling all exceptional conditions. Exceptions which occur with low dynamic frequency are then handled using software assistance.

The MIPS architecture provides the necessary information and interrupts for trapping on exception conditions, but relies extensively on software to implement the IEEE recommendations for support of floating-point exception trap handlers.

IEEE Exception Trapping

The IEEE floating-point standard makes recommendations on information to be made available during a floating-point exception trap handler. This information often includes the original operand values or other information which must be computed in hardware unless the original operand values are retained.

All of the information which the trap handler must determine can be derived from the state of the floating-point coprocessor at the time of the trap. However, in order to provide significant simplifications in the complexity of the FPA, some computation may need to be performed within the trap handler of an associated software envelope to determine the information.

IEEE Format Compatibility

The IEEE standard requires a 32-bit floating-point format (single), and recommends a 64-bit floating-point format (double).

The MIPS floating-point architecture uses the IEEE standard single-precision and double-precision floating-point formats.

The IEEE standard does not specify the exact format of the extended format and the R2010 does not implement, nor does UMIPS software support, this format.

Implementing IEEE Standard Operations in Software

Some of the operations required or recommended by the IEEE standard are not provided directly by the FPA. These operations are not implemented in the floating-point instruction set either because of their high complexity, low frequency of use, or redundancy with the set of implemented instructions. The paragraphs that follow provide code descriptions and skeletons for the implementation of some of these operations.

Remainder

The *remainder* function is accomplished by repeated magnitude subtraction of a scaled form of the divisor, until the dividend/remainder is one-half of the divisor or until the magnitude is less than one-half of the magnitude of the divisor. The scaling of the divisor ensures that each subtraction step is exact; thus the remainder function itself is always exact. This function is provided in the routine *drem()* in libm.a of the UMIPS compiler release for the double-precision format. See the manual page *IEEE(3M)* in the appropriate UMIPS system reference manual.

Round to Integer

The *round to integer in floating-point format* function may be implemented by adding a fudge factor that causes normal rounding to occur at the end of the floating-point fraction, and then subtracting it back again. The code example below is for single-precision; the double-precision version is similar. This function is provided in the routine *rint()* in libm.a of the UMIPS compiler release for the double-precision format. See the manual page *floor(3M)* in the appropriate UMIPS system reference manual.

```
;  Single-precision round to integer
;  Operand is in f0
;  Result placed in f0
;  Registers f2, f4 modified
   lwc1      f2,16777216.0e0     ;f2 ← 2 24
   abs.s     f4,f0               ;f4 ← |f0|
   fc.ole.s  f2,f4               ;f2 ? ≤ f4
   bc1f      1f                  ;leave alone if NaN, infinity or ≥ 2 24
   c.eq.s    f0,f4               ;was f0 negative?
   bc1t      2f                  ;Yes → will have to negate result
   add.s     f4,f2,f4            ;round off to integer
   j         1f                  ;all done after one more instruction
   sub.s     f0,f4,f2            ;remove fudge factor
2:
   sub.s     f0,f2,f4            ;remove fudge factor and negate
1:
```

Convert between Binary and Decimal

These functions are provided in the routines *atof(3)* and *printf(3)* in libc.a of the UMIPS releases. See the manual page *atof(3)* and *printf(3)* in the appropriate UMIPS system reference manual.

Copy Sign

The *copy sign* operation can be performed using floating–point compares and the absolute value and negation operations. Special attention must be paid to negative zero, as it has negative sign, but zero value. This function is provided in the routine *copysign()* in libm.a of the UMIPS releases. See the manual page *IEEE(3)* in the appropriate UMIPS system reference manual.

Scale Binary

This operation is performed by moving the operand to the processor, where shift and add operations perform the basic operation. Checking for exceptional operands can be performed in either the processor or the floating–point coprocessor. This function is provided in the routine *scalb()* in libm.a of the UMIPS releases. See the manual page *IEEE(3M)* in the appropriate UMIPS system reference manual.

Log Binary

This operation is performed by moving the operand to the processor, where shift and add operations perform the basic operation. This function is provided in the routine *logb()* in libm.a of the UMIPS releases. See the manual page *IEEE(3M)* in the appropriate UMIPS system reference manual.

Next After

This operation is performed by comparing the two floating–point values to determine the direction to compute the neighbor, then moving the operand to the processor, where single–precision or multiple–precision add operations perform the basic operation.

Finite

This operation can be provided by taking the absolute value and comparing for equality with $+\infty$. This function is provided in the routine *finite()* in libm.a of the UMIPS releases. See the manual page *IEEE(3M)* in the appropriate UMIPS system reference manual.

Is NaN

This operation is provided by using the unordered predicates of the floating–point compare operation.

Arithmetic Inequality

This operation is available as the floating–point compare operation.

Class

This operation is performed by moving the operand to the processor, where fixed–point shifts and comparisons can classify the floating–point value. These functions are provided in the routines *fp_class_d()* and *fp_class_f()* in libc.a of the UMIPS releases. See the manual page *fp_class(3)* in the appropriate UMIPS system reference manual.

Index

G

H

I

V

V (invalid operation) exception, FPA 8–5
V (Valid) bit 4–6
values, calculating in FP format 6–9
variable instruction execution time 1–6
vector locations, exceptions 5–12
virtual address, bad (BadVAddr) register 5–10
virtual address format 4–1
virtual address translation 4–7, 4–8
virtual addressing,
   kernal mode 4–3
   virtual memory and the TLB 4–4
virtual memory map 4–2
virtual memory segments 2–11, 4–3
virtual memory system 1–17
virtual page number (see VPN)
VPN (Virtual Page Number) 4–1, 4–6, 5–10

W

write buffer 2–14
write indexed TLB entry A–83
write random TLB entry (TLBWR) A–84
write TLB instruction (TLBW) 4–11

X

XOR (exclusive OR) A–85
XORI (exclusive OR immediate) A–86

Z

Z (division–by–zero) exception, FPA 8–6
zan (see author)
zero, floating–point 6–11
zero parity (PZ) bit, Status register 5–7